REALISM IN OUR TIME

Literature and the Class Struggle

REALISM IN OUR TIME

Literature and the Class Struggle

GEORG LUKÁCS

With a preface by
GEORGE STEINER

HARPER TORCHBOOKS
Harper & Row, Publishers
New York, Evanston, San Francisco, London

Translated from the German by
John and Necke Mander

This Torchbook paperback edition reprints Volume XXXIII of the
WORLD PERSPECTIVES series, which is planned and edited by RUTH NANDA
ANSHEN. Dr. Anshen's Epilogue to this reprint appears on page 137.

First HARPER TORCHBOOK edition published 1971

STANDARD BOOK NUMBER: 06-131603-2

Contents

GEORG LUKÁCS—A PREFACE *by George Steiner*   7

I.   THE IDEOLOGY OF MODERNISM   17

II.   FRANZ KAFKA OR THOMAS MANN?   47

III.   CRITICAL REALISM AND SOCIALIST REALISM   93

EPILOGUE *by Ruth Nanda Anshen*   137

Georg Lukács—A Preface

THE CASE of Georg Lukács offers a complex, powerful instance of the conditions of spirit in our time. His work has been performed under the stress of ideological conflict and political crisis. It is committed to that stress. Lukács believes that the work of art and the statement of thought— where they are responsible human actions, rooted in human need—are inseparable from the historical and political context. Hence the polemic and deliberately occasional quality of much of his writing. Lukács argues that there are books which are intensely necessary at a certain focus or moment in society but which should strive to resolve the problems they engage and thus carry in them their own oblivion. To write 'for eternity' is a romantic posture. It is the more ironic that *History and Class Consciousness* (1923)—a book Lukács has repudiated, not out of political fear, but because he genuinely believes that it misinterprets fundamental notions of dialectical materialism —should endure as the most famous and subversive of his achievements.

But this ambiguity is inherent. Since his transition from Hegelian historicism to thorough Marxism in 1917–1920, Lukács has found himself hammering out and defending a position which is both central and unorthodox. He is, after Marx, Engels and Plekhanov, the only major philosophic talent to have emerged from the crucible of Hegelian theory and communist fact. But his creative life has been conditioned by the pressure and falsehood of Stalinist rule. Lukács has striven, with formidable courage and intellectual resource, to keep alive, during the long winter of terror and cliché, the central impulse of Marxist criticism and radical hope.

He survived by tactics of indirect reference. It is his implicit refusal to deal, other than perfunctorily, with Soviet and 'pro-

7

gressive' literature of the Stalinist era, and his determination to write, instead, of Goethe, Balzac, Stendhal, Heine, Pushkin, Thomas Mann, that constitute Lukács's essential critique. So far as Soviet society has refuted Stalinist practice, and is allowing both in Russia and Eastern Europe a measure of debate and artistic experiment, Lukács's stubborn optimism has been vindicated. The question of whether dialectical materialism and a communist organization of the means of production must degenerate, necessarily, into totalitarian rule is, at least, open.

To that vital indecision, Lukács has contributed tremendously. Even where it is clandestine, his influence is profound. Without the revaluation of Hegel and the vision of historical process developed in *History and Class Consciousness,* French existentialism is hardly conceivable. Sartre's concept of *engagement*—the commitment of art and the individual to the exigencies of political and social conflict, the realization of individual consciousness through the concrete, historical situation —derives largely from Lukács. It is the subtle, tenacious insinuation of Lukács's philosophic radicalism that has given the Italian communist movement something of its humane generosity and cunning to resist the dead hand of Stalinism. Wherever Marxism has engendered independent, heretical life—in Adorno's sociology of music, in the utopian poetics of Ernest Bloch, in Walter Benjamin's brilliant study of technological means and aesthetic forms, in Lucien Goldmann's analysis of the interactions of class and metaphysics in French drama— Lukács's voice and presence have given the initial impulse. During the time of hideous provincialism and banality imposed by Nazism on the German language and on German intellectual life, Lukács, writing in exile, sought to define the roots of the catastrophe (*The Destruction of Reason*), and to shore up against ruin the legacy of German literature (*Gottfried Keller,* 1940; *Goethe and His Time,* 1947; *Thomas Mann,* 1949; *German Realists of the XIXth Century,* 1951).

8

Today, an awareness of Lukács is the touchstone of alertness in Eastern Europe.

The English or American reader will not find Lukács's work easy of access. Its sheer mass poses difficulties, and only a handful of the thirty books and fifty essays and articles has, so far, been translated. Lukács assumes a certain familiarity with the vocabulary and argument of German metaphysics, from Kant and Hegel to Fichte and Schopenhauer. But it is a plain, though disturbing fact that Anglo-Saxon literacy has remained generally ignorant of a body of thought from which have sprung much of the creative complication and nightmare of present history. Moreover, Lukács presupposes that his reader will have some notion of the classic lineage of Marxism, of the doctrines and revisions that lead from Hegel and Feuerbach to Kautsky, Mehring, Plekhanov. Lukács's style and strategy of persuasion are steeped in the special tone and fabric of Marxist debate. We cannot read Aquinas without some inkling of the scholastic mode, or Rousseau as if Hobbes and Locke had not written before him. Here again, however, there is a dilemma of language; many of the canonic philosophic and Marxist texts on which Lukács founds his argument are, as yet, available only in German. Finally, there is the crucial accident of Lukács's own style.

He writes obscurely, or with a certain close-meshed, inelegant force, because he believes that criticism and philosophic discourse should differ from *belles lettres,* that the critic who seeks to make of his essay an artistic performance is merely betraying his envy of the writer. He writes in an uncompromising prose, bristling with technical qualifications and cross-reference, because he feels that the problems engaged *are* difficult, that we betray where we simplify or sacrifice to ease of presentation the gray, intricate obstinacies of the truth. Like Spinoza, moreover, Lukács has wrought for himself a language of inner emigration and exile. Though he grew up in Budapest, he wrote only two early works in Hungarian. After 1910, he adopted German, the *lingua franca* of European socialism and post-Hegelian ideology. Between 1933 and 1945, a time in which he composed much of his finest criticism, Lukács lived as a refugee in Moscow, on the dangerous fringe of Stalinist suspicion. Increasingly, his German assumed the habits of exile, the stiffness and inward allusion of a language cut off from the roughage of living speech. In 1945, he returned to Budapest, where he still lives, in a great cell of books high above the river. Here, also, his use of German is both a safeguard of independence and a symptom of isolation. In short, he has made of his language a citadel, and one needs patience at the gate.

But once we enter, there is God's plenty. Among critics, only Sainte-Beuve and Edmund Wilson have matched the breadth of Lukács's response. His heritage is central European, with the literal implication of that which is at the centre, and of a central tradition. A pupil of Max Weber and Simmel, Lukács was steeped in the historical and philological erudition distinctive of German social theory. His roots go back to Aristotle and the Stoics; he is profoundly at home in European and Russian literature. Like Marx himself, Lukács derives much of the tenor of his sensibility from the masters of eighteenth-century humanism, Voltaire, Diderot, Goethe. From the start, his preoccupation with the theory of the novel led him to an equal study of Cervantes and Balzac, of Dickens and Manzoni, of Thomas Mann and Tolstoy. There is in the achievement of Lukács, as in that of Marx, a distinctively Jewish disregard of national or linguistic barriers, and a sense of history and spiritual form as transcendent energies.

From this massive, close-argued body of work, it is almost impossible to select any one strand and say 'Here is Lukács at his best.' The local insight or contention interlocks vitally with the totality of Lukács's own thought, and with the larger sphere of Hegelian-Marxist vision. Moreover, Lukács has been continually revising and correcting his own discernments. Self-criticism and self-censorship are not, primarily, the result of Stalinist terror. They represent the effort of the individual

Marxist to act out, in his own life and thinking, the organic and historical process of dialectics. Contradiction moves toward synthesis, synthesis splinters into new and creative contradiction. The individual book or essay is a provisional segment—a taking stock—along the continuous path of dialectical inquiry. Furthermore (and this is crucial to Lukács's indictment of Nietzsche), a writer is responsible for all potential misreadings or distortions of his text. No sentence must be allowed to stand if it could, in a changed historical setting, be used to evil or false purpose. Thus it is better to withdraw or even burn books than to let them be subverted.

Nevertheless, and in disregard of the surrounding methodological and philosophic material, a number of specific critical achievements can be singled out.

Already in *The Theory of the Novel,* a pre-Marxist essay which established his early fame, Lukács sought to define the relationship between prose fiction and social reality, between the novel and time seen as concrete, historical medium. On that relationship depend essential discriminations between the three principal genres of Western literature: the epic, drama, and prose fiction. Marxism, to which we owe the analysis of the rise of the modern novel out of a mercantile ethic and against the background of a nascent urban middle-class, sharpened Lukács's concern with the interaction of time and prose narrative. The result is one of his finest works, *The Historical Novel* (1955).

Lukács shows that the form embodies a crisis in European sensibility. The French Revolution and the Napoleonic era informed the consciousness of ordinary men—whose lives had been hitherto essentially domestic or outside history—with a new sense of historical involvement. The private individual was drawn into the stress of history by the totalitarian claims of social insurrection and warfare on a popular or national rather than professional, mercenary scale. Sweeping across Europe, the revolutionary and Napoleonic armies, unlike their eighteenth-century predecessors, politicized the very fabric of

11

daily life. History was no longer a matter for archives and princes. To this change, Scott's *Waverley* novels gave direct and prophetic response. The mob scene in *The Heart of Mid-lothian* or the image of Glasgow in *Rob Roy* represents an entirely new observance of the weight and complexity of historical fact. Lukács was the first to show this.

He goes on to explore the modes of historical fiction in Manzoni, Pushkin, Victor Hugo and Thackeray. He argues that the historical novel falters when the writer no longer experiences a rational continuity between the past and his own time, when the social forces among which he lives seem to him beyond comprehension or control. In protest, the historical novelist turns to increasingly remote or exotic themes. Instead of fiction, of life realized by force of imaginative recognition, we find laboured archaeology. Lukács draws the dividing line in 1848 and enforces the contrast between *The Charterhouse of Parma,* with its vivid, rational presentment of historical and political conflict, and the inert artifice of Flaubert's *Salammbô.*

This judgment, to which Lukács brings a weight of close, critical argument, reflects one of his primary theses. Inquiring into the marvellous concreteness of Homer, into the life and sensual immediacy with which classic art is able to instil material objects, Hegel sketched a theory of *alienation.* As the techniques of production become more specialized and anonymous, as the modes of daily existence grow more splintered and artificial (the modern city), the imaginations of poet and reader lose their grip on the vital particularity of physical and material processes. Capitalism and mass production, in which the individual worker neither sees the rational totality of the operation nor cares about the integrity of the individual artifact, severs man from the natural rhythms and shapes of creation. Whereas Ulysses—and those who listened to Homer's epic—could build the rafts they sailed upon, we are mere users of objects and techniques which we have not ourselves mastered or truly understood. How many modern city dwellers could give a coherent account of how their bread is baked?

Man lives as a harried guest in the world, and primary human relations become abstract expressions of economic control or economic dependence. This is what the Marxist calls *Verdinglichung,* the 're-ification' of life.

Lukács has applied these deep, intricate notions to the problem of the decline of the French novel after Stendhal. From this particular instance derives his generalized concept of the decay from *realism* to *naturalism.* The realist—Balzac, Stendhal—exhibits an immediate, unworried grasp of material fact. As capitalism grows more oppressive and the artist feels more alien to his society, this grasp changes to an anxious rapacity. Flaubert attempts to recapture the real by force of accumulated detail and technical language. The words become not the voice but the inventory of experience. When Balzac describes a hat, he does so because a man is wearing it. The famous account of Charles Bovary's cap, with its fantastic accumulation of sartorial terms, is a piece of hollow bravado. Where the realist selects, the naturalist enumerates (Zola's catalogue of cheeses in *Le Ventre de Paris*). The breath of life is gone and the novel declines to photographic reportage. We move from the world of Balzac to that of Studs Lonigan. Note how Lukács's critical scruple plays against the demands of propaganda or party dogma. He exalts Balzac, a man of royalist and clerical principles; he condemns Zola, a political 'progressive' and forerunner of 'socialist realism.' This is precisely why the police-dogs of Stalinist culture have always bayed at Lukács's heels and sniffed treason. Writing in 1954, Joseph Revai, Hungary's version of Zhdanov, turned bitterly on his former teacher:

> What could Hungarian literature gain from the pass-word given it by Lukács in 1945: "Zola? No, Balzac!" And what could it gain from the slogan put forward by Lukács in 1948: "Neither Pirandello nor Priestley, but Shakespeare and Molière"? In both instances—nothing.

At a time when German literary criticism led a servile or insignificant existence, Lukács's work stood pre-eminent. He

13

proceeds in the manner of a hawk. The particular book or writer serves as point of departure. From it Lukács's argument moves outward, traversing large, complex ground. But the central idea or query is kept constantly in view. Finally, the dialectic closes in, marshalling its examples and persuasions. Thus the long essay on the Goethe-Schiller correspondence deals with the problem of the nature and limits of literary forms. The discussion of Hölderlin's *Hyperion* gives rise to a review of the ambiguous role of the Hellenic ideal in the history of the German spirit. In his several essays on Thomas Mann, Lukács tries to define the paradox of the bourgeois artist in a century of revolution and overthrow. He argues that Mann's stoic irony, his experiments with archaic motifs and styles show that Mann, although he has chosen to stay outside the stream of history, is aware of the tragic and futile nature of his choice. Mann, in turn, long regarded Lukács as the greatest of his critics and left a brilliant portrait of him under the guise of Naphta in *The Magic Mountain*. Lukács's monograph on Gottfried Keller is an attempt to clarify the very difficult problem of the arrested development in German literature after the death of Goethe.

All this is but to scratch the surface. The complete edition, now in progress, will fill some twenty large volumes. The long-awaited *Aesthetik* is shortly to be published. Obviously, it will take time before Lukács's achievement can be seen as a whole, before the parts of insight and of blindness can be justly separated.

There is blindness. Lukács is weak on poetry, partly because he lacks 'ear'—the faculty that Ezra Pound or Empson has to choose, on the instant, the note of glory in a poem—partly because he distrusts all extreme and private uses of language. He is committed to the axiom that the greatest styles (he would name Socrates, Christ, Lenin) are also the simplest and most translatable. Lukács believes that where language grows autonomous, where it sets its music in the place of clear meaning, the writer is betraying his task. He has said nothing just of

14

Rilke, Yeats, Eliot or Valéry. Only Hölderlin troubles him; here Lukács does seem to perceive the responsibilities and integrity of lyricism.

Lukács is a radical moralist. Like Victorian critics, he tends to condemn art whose themes he finds unsavoury, or in which man is shown in the light of obsession or weakness. Hence his insensitivity to Dostoevsky and his failure to grasp the real scope of Proust. The luxuriance and perversities of which Proust builds his tragic vision outrage Lukács's ascetic, optimistic morality. He does not see that in Proust the classic energies of the French novel come to their natural unfolding, or that Proust's irony gives as severe an indictment of his society as does that of Mann. Similar motives are at work in his rejection of Joyce. To Lukács, the saga of Bloom is merely *petit-bourgeois* narcissism run mad. In this great Marxist, there is an old-style puritan.

But it is not the particular omission or persuasive insight that constitutes Lukács's essential quality. His greatness is a matter of inner stance, of *tone*. Wherever we accede to this large enterprise of criticism and philosophic argument, the sense of a supreme seriousness, of a complete trust in the life of the imagination and of thought, overwhelms. Against exile and Stalinism, against broken hope and solitude, this man has set the power of the word. Lukács's inheritance is richer than Marxism; it goes back to the radical espousal of intelligence, to the unflinching humanism of Aristotle. Entering Lukács's study, in a house scarred by war, one has the sensation of ideas palpably alive and burning. At moments, we may feel driven back or bewildered by the twist of flame. But the warmth is real.

GEORGE STEINER

The Ideology of Modernism

IT IS in no way surprising that the most influential contemporary school of writing should still be committed to the dogmas of 'modernist' anti-realism. It is here that we must begin our investigation if we are to chart the possibilities of a bourgeois realism. We must compare the two main trends in contemporary bourgeois literature, and look at the answers they give to the major ideological and artistic questions of our time.

We shall concentrate on the underlying ideological basis of these trends (ideological in the above-defined, not in the strictly philosophical, sense). What must be avoided at all costs is the approach generally adopted by bourgeois-modernist critics themselves: that exaggerated concern with formal criteria, with questions of style and literary technique. This approach may appear to distinguish sharply between 'modern' and 'traditional' writing (i.e. contemporary writers who adhere to the styles of the last century). In fact it fails to locate the decisive formal problems and turns a blind eye to their inherent dialectic. We are presented with a false polarization which, by exaggerating the importance of stylistic differences, conceals the opposing principles actually underlying and determining contrasting styles.

To take an example: the *monologue intérieur*. Compare, for instance, Bloom's monologue in the lavatory or Molly's monologue in bed, at the beginning and at the end of *Ulysses*, with Goethe's early-morning monologue as conceived by Thomas Mann in his *Lotte in Weimar*. Plainly, the same stylistic technique is being employed. And certain of Thomas Mann's remarks about Joyce and his methods would appear to confirm this.

Yet it is not easy to think of any two novels more basically dissimilar than *Ulysses* and *Lotte in Weimar*. This is true even

17

of the superficially rather similar scenes I have indicated. I am not referring to the—to my mind—striking difference in intellectual quality. I refer to the fact that with Joyce the stream-of-consciousness technique is no mere stylistic device; it is itself the formative principle governing the narrative pattern and the presentation of character. Technique here is something absolute; it is part and parcel of the aesthetic ambition informing *Ulysses*. With Thomas Mann, on the other hand, the *monologue intérieur* is simply a technical device, allowing the author to explore aspects of Goethe's world which would not have been otherwise available. Goethe's experience is not presented as confined to momentary sense-impressions. The artist reaches down to the core of Goethe's personality, to the complexity of his relations with his own past, present, and even future experience. The stream of association is only apparently free. The monologue is composed with the utmost artistic rigour: it is a carefully plotted sequence gradually piercing to the core of Goethe's personality. Every person or event, emerging momentarily from the stream and vanishing again, is given a specific weight, a definite position, in the pattern of the whole. However unconventional the presentation, the compositional principle is that of the traditional epic; in the way the pace is controlled, and the transitions and climaxes are organized, the ancient rules of epic narration are faithfully observed.

It would be absurd, in view of Joyce's artistic ambitions and his manifest abilities, to qualify the exaggerated attention he gives to the detailed recording of sense-data, and his comparative neglect of ideas and emotions, as artistic failure. All this was in conformity with Joyce's artistic intentions; and, by use of such techniques, he may be said to have achieved them satisfactorily. But between Joyce's intentions and those of Thomas Mann there is a total opposition. The perpetually oscillating patterns of sense- and memory-data, their powerfully charged—but aimless and directionless—fields of force, give rise to an epic structure which is *static,* reflecting a belief in the basically static character of events.

18

These opposed views of the world—dynamic and developmental on the one hand, static and sensational on the other—are of crucial importance in examining the two schools of literature I have mentioned. I shall return to the opposition later. Here, I want only to point out that an exclusive emphasis on formal matters can lead to serious misunderstanding of the character of an artist's work.

What determines the style of a given work of art? How does the intention determine the form? (We are concerned here, of course, with the intention realized in the work; it need not coincide with the writer's conscious intention). The distinctions that concern us are not those between stylistic 'techniques' in the formalistic sense. It is the view of the world, the ideology or *weltanschauung* underlying a writer's work, that counts. And it is the writer's attempt to reproduce this view of the world which constitutes his 'intention' and is the formative principle underlying the style of a given piece of writing. Looked at in this way, style ceases to be a formalistic category. Rather, it is rooted in content; it is the specific form of a specific content.

Content determines form. But there is no content of which Man himself is not the focal point. However various the *données* of literature (a particular experience, a didactic purpose), the basic question is, and will remain: what is Man?

Here is a point of division: if we put the question in abstract, philosophical terms, leaving aside all formal considerations, we arrive—for the realist school—at the traditional Aristotelian dictum (which was also reached by other than purely aesthetic considerations): Man is *zoon politikon*, a social animal. The Aristotelian dictum is applicable to all great realistic literature. Achilles and Werther, Oedipus and Tom Jones, Antigone and Anna Karenina: their individual existence—their *Sein an sich*, in the Hegelian terminology; their 'ontological being', as a more fashionable terminology has it—cannot be distinguished from their social and historical environment. Their human significance, their specific individuality cannot be separated from the context in which they were created.

19

but isn't this rel. to the
particular historical
environment that would
breed this.

The ontological view governing the image of man in the work of leading modernist writers is the exact opposite of this. Man, for these writers, is by nature solitary, asocial, unable to enter into relationships with other human beings. Thomas Wolfe once wrote: 'My view of the world is based on the firm conviction that solitariness is by no means a rare condition, something peculiar to myself or to a few specially solitary human beings, but the inescapable, central fact of human existence.' Man, thus imagined, may establish contact with other individuals, but only in a superficial, accidental manner; only, ontologically speaking, by retrospective reflection. For 'the others', too, are basically solitary, beyond significant human relationship.

This basic solitariness of man must not be confused with that individual solitariness to be found in the literature of traditional realism. In the latter case, we are dealing with a particular situation in which a human being may be placed, due either to his character or to the circumstances of his life. Solitariness may be objectively conditioned, as with Sophocles' Philoctetes, put ashore on the bleak island of Lemnos. Or it may be subjective, the product of inner necessity, as with Tolstoy's Ivan Ilyitsch or Flaubert's Frédéric Moreau in the *Education Sentimentale*. But it is always merely a fragment, a phase, a climax or anti-climax, in the life of the community as a whole. The fate of such individuals is characteristic of certain human types in specific social or historical circumstances. Beside and beyond their solitariness, the common life, the strife and togetherness of other human beings, goes on as before. In a word, their solitariness is a specific social fate, not a universal *condition humaine*.

The latter, of course, is characteristic of the theory and practice of modernism. I would like, in the present study, to spare the reader tedious excursions into philosophy. But I cannot refrain from drawing the reader's attention to Heidegger's description of human existence as a 'thrownness-into-being' (*Geworfenheit ins Dasein*). A more graphic evocation of the ontological solitariness of the individual would be hard to imagine. Man is 'thrown-into-being'. This implies, not merely that man is constitutionally

20

Does Joyce compensate by ch. context?

unable to establish relationships with things or persons outside himself; but also that it is impossible to determine theoretically the origin and goal of human existence.

Man, thus conceived, is an ahistorical being. (The fact that Heidegger does admit a form of 'authentic' historicity in his system is not really relevant. I have shown elsewhere that Heidegger tends to belittle historicity as 'vulgar'; and his 'authentic' historicity is not distinguishable from ahistoricity). This negation of history takes two different forms in modernist literature. First, the hero is strictly confined within the limits of his own experience. There is not for him—and apparently not for his creator—any pre-existent reality beyond his own self, acting upon him or being acted upon by him. Secondly, the hero himself is without personal history. He is 'thrown-into-the-world': meaninglessly, unfathomably. He does not develop through contact with the world; he neither forms nor is formed by it. The only 'development' in this literature is the gradual revelation of the human condition. Man is now what he has always been and always will be. The narrator, the examining subject, is in motion; the examined reality is static.

Of course, dogmas of this kind are only really viable in philosophical abstraction, and then only with a measure of sophistry. A gifted writer, however extreme his theoretical modernism, will in practice have to compromise with the demands of historicity and of social environment. Joyce uses Dublin, Kafka and Musil the Hapsburg Monarchy, as the locus of their masterpieces. But the locus they lovingly depict is little more than a backcloth; it is not basic to their artistic intention.

This view of human existence has specific literary consequences. Particularly in one category, of primary theoretical and practical importance, to which we must now give our attention: that of *potentiality*. Philosophy distinguishes between *abstract* and *concrete* (in Hegel, 'real') *potentiality*. These two categories, their interrelation and opposition, are rooted in life itself. *Potentiality*—seen abstractly or subjectively—is richer than actual life. Innumerable possibilities for man's development

21

are imaginable, only a small percentage of which will be realized. Modern subjectivism, taking these imagined possibilities for actual complexity of life, oscillates between melancholy and fascination. When the world declines to realize these possibilities, this melancholy becomes tinged with contempt. Hofmannsthal's Sobeide expressed the reaction of the generation first exposed to this experience:

> The burden of those endlessly pored-over
> And now forever perished possibilities . . .

How far were those possibilities even concrete or 'real'? Plainly, they existed only in the imagination of the subject, as dreams or day-dreams. Faulkner, in whose work this subjective potentiality plays an important part, was evidently aware that reality must thereby be subjectivized and made to appear arbitrary. Consider this comment of his: 'They were all talking simultaneously, getting flushed and excited, quarrelling, making the unreal into a possibility, then into a probability, then into an irrefutable fact, as human beings do when they put their wishes into words.' The possibilities in a man's mind, the particular pattern, intensity and suggestiveness they assume, will of course be characteristic of that individual. In practice, their number will border on the infinite, even with the most unimaginative individual. It is thus a hopeless undertaking to define the contours of individuality, let alone to come to grips with a man's actual fate, by means of potentiality. The *abstract* character of potentiality is clear from the fact that it cannot determine development—subjective mental states, however permanent or profound, cannot here be decisive. Rather, the development of personality is determined by inherited gifts and qualities; by the factors, external or internal, which further or inhibit their growth.

But in life potentiality can, of course, become reality. Situations arise in which a man is confronted with a choice; and in the act of choice a man's character may reveal itself in a light that surprises even himself. In literature—and particularly in

22

dramatic literature—the denouement often consists in the realization of just such a potentiality, which circumstances have kept from coming to the fore. These potentialities are, then, 'real' or concrete potentialities. The fate of the character depends upon the potentiality in question, even if it should condemn him to a tragic end. In advance, while still a subjective potentiality in the character's mind, there is no way of distinguishing it from the innumerable abstract potentialities in his mind. It may even be buried away so completely that, before the moment of decision, it has never entered his mind even as an abstract potentiality. The subject, after taking his decision, may be un-conscious of his own motives. Thus Richard Dudgeon, Shaw's Devil's Disciple, having sacrificed himself as Pastor Andersen, confesses: 'I have often asked myself for the motive, but I find no good reason to explain why I acted as I did.'

Yet it is a decision which has altered the direction of his life. Of course, this is an extreme case. But the qualitative leap of the denouement, cancelling and at the same time renewing the continuity of individual consciousness, can never be predicted. The concrete potentiality cannot be isolated from the myriad abstract potentialities. Only actual decision reveals the distinction.

The literature of realism, aiming at a truthful reflection of reality, must demonstrate both the concrete and abstract potentialities of human beings in extreme situations of this kind. A character's concrete potentiality once revealed, his abstract potentialities will appear essentially inauthentic. Moravia, for instance, in his novel *The Indifferent Ones*, describes the young son of a decadent bourgeois family, Michel, who makes up his mind to kill his sister's seducer. While Michel, having made his decision, is planning the murder, a large number of abstract—but highly suggestive—possibilities are laid before us. Unfortunately for Michel the murder is actually carried out; and, from the sordid details of the action, Michel's character emerges as what it is—representative of that background from which, in subjective fantasy, he had imagined he could escape.

Abstract potentiality belongs wholly to the realm of subjecttivity; whereas concrete potentiality is concerned with the dialectic between the individual's subjectivity and objective reality. The literary presentation of the latter thus implies a description of actual persons inhabiting a palpable, identifiable world. Only in the interaction of character and environment can the concrete potentiality of a particular individual be singled out from the 'bad infinity' of purely abstract potentialities, and emerge as the determining potentiality of just this individual at just this phase of his development. This principle alone enables the artist to distinguish concrete potentiality from a myriad abstractions.

But the ontology on which the image of man in modernist literature is based invalidates this principle. If the 'human condition'—man as a solitary being, incapable of meaningful relationships—is identified with reality itself, the distinction between abstract and concrete potentiality becomes null and void. The categories tend to merge. Thus Cesare Pavese notes with John Dos Passos, and his German contemporary, Alfred Döblin, a sharp oscillation between 'superficial *verisme*' and 'abstract Expressionist schematism'. Criticizing Dos Passos, Pavese writes that fictional characters 'ought to be created by deliberate selection and description of individual features'—implying that Dos Passos' characterizations are transferable from one individual to another. He describes the artistic consequences: by exalting man's subjectivity, at the expense of the objective reality of his environment, man's subjectivity itself is impoverished.

The problem, once again, is ideological. This is not to say that the ideology underlying modernist writings is identical in all cases. On the contrary: the ideology exists in extremely various, even contradictory forms. The rejection of narrative objectivity, the surrender to subjectivity, may take the form of Joyce's stream of consciousness, or of Musil's 'active passivity', his 'existence without quality', or of Gide's *action gratuite*', where abstract potentiality achieves pseudo-realization. As individual character manifests itself in life's moments of decision, so too in literature. If the distinction between abstract and concrete potentiality vanishes, if man's inwardness is identified with an abstract subjectivity, human personality must necessarily disintegrate.

T. S. Eliot described this phenomenon, this mode of portraying human personality, as

> Shape without form, shade without colour,
> Paralysed force, gesture without motion.

The disintegration of personality is matched by a disintegration of the outer world. In one sense, this is simply a further consequence of our argument. For the identification of abstract and concrete human potentiality rests on the assumption that the objective world is inherently inexplicable. Certain leading modernist writers, attempting a theoretical apology, have admitted this quite frankly. Often this theoretical impossibility of understanding reality is the point of departure, rather than the exaltation of subjectivity. But in any case the connection between the two is plain. The German poet Gottfried Benn, for instance, informs us that 'there is no outer reality, there is only human consciousness, constantly building, modifying, rebuilding new worlds out of its own creativity'. Musil, as always, gives a moral twist to this line of thought. Ulrich, the hero of his *The Man without Qualities*, when asked what he would do if he were in God's place, replies: 'I should be compelled to abolish reality.' Subjective existence 'without qualities' is the complement of the negation of outward reality.

The negation of outward reality is not always demanded with such theoretical rigour. But it is present in almost all modernist literature. In conversation, Musil once gave as the period of his great novel, 'between 1912 and 1914'. But he was quick to modify this statement by adding: 'I have not, I must insist, written a historical novel. I am not concerned with actual events. . . . Events, anyhow, are interchangeable. I am interested in what is typical, in what one might call the ghostly aspect of reality.' The word 'ghostly' is interesting. It points to a major tendency in modernist literature: the attenuation of actuality. In Kafka, the descriptive detail is of an extraordinary immediacy and

25

authenticity. But Kafka's artistic ingenuity is really directed towards substituting his *angst*-ridden vision of the world for objective reality. The realistic detail is the expression of a ghostly un-reality, of a nightmare world, whose function is to evoke *angst*. The same phenomenon can be seen in writers who attempt to combine Kafka's techniques with a critique of society—like the German writer, Wolfgang Koeppen, in his satirical novel about Bonn, *Das Treibhaus*. A similar attenuation of reality underlies Joyce's stream of consciousness. It is, of course, intensified where the stream of consciousness is itself the medium through which reality is presented. And it is carried *ad absurdum* where the stream of consciousness is that of an abnormal subject or of an idiot—consider the first part of Faulkner's *Sound and Fury* or, a still more extreme case, Beckett's *Molloy*.

Attenuation of reality and dissolution of personality are thus interdependent: the stronger the one, the stronger the other. Underlying both is the lack of a consistent view of human nature. Man is reduced to a sequence of unrelated experiential fragments; he is as inexplicable to others as to himself. In Eliot's *Cocktail Party* the psychiatrist, who voices the opinions of the author, describes the phenomenon:

> Ah, but we die to each other daily
> What we know of other people
> Is only our memory of the moments
> During which we knew them. And they have changed
> since then.
> To pretend that they and we are the same
> Is a useful and convenient social convention
> Which must sometimes be broken. We must also remember
> That at every meeting we are meeting a stranger.

The dissolution of personality, originally the unconscious product of the identification of concrete and abstract potentiality, is elevated to a deliberate principle in the light of consciousness. It is no accident that Gottfried Benn called one of his theoretical tracts 'Doppelleben'. For Benn, this dissolution of personality

26

took the form of a schizophrenic dichotomy. According to him, there was in man's personality no coherent pattern of motivation or behaviour. Man's animal nature is opposed to his denaturized, sublimated thought-processes. The unity of thought and action is 'backwoods philosophy'; thought and being are 'quite separate entities'. Man must be either a moral or a thinking being—he cannot be both at once.

These are not, I think, purely private, eccentric speculations. Of course, they are derived from Benn's specific experience. But there is an inner connection between these ideas and a certain tradition of bourgeois thought. It is more than a hundred years since Kierkegaard first attacked the Hegelian view that the inner and outer world form an objective dialectical unity, that they are indissolubly married in spite of their apparent opposition. Kierkegaard denied any such unity. According to Kierkegaard, the individual exists within an opaque, impenetrable 'incognito'.

This philosophy attained remarkable popularity after the Second World War—proof that even the most abstruse theories may reflect social reality. Men like Martin Heidegger, Ernst Jünger, the lawyer Carl Schmitt, Gottfried Benn and others passionately embraced this doctrine of the eternal incognito which implies that a man's external deeds are no guide to his motives. In this case, the deeds obscured behind the mysterious incognito were, needless to say, these intellectuals' participation in Nazism: Heidegger, as Rector of Freiburg University, had glorified Hitler's seizure of power at his Inauguration; Carl Schmitt had put his great legal gifts at Hitler's disposal. The facts were too well-known to be simply denied. But, if this impenetrable incognito were the true *condition humaine*, might not—concealed within their incognito—Heidegger or Schmitt have been secret opponents of Hitler all the time, only supporting him in the world of appearances? Ernst von Salomon's cynical frankness about his opportunism in The Questionnaire (keeping his reservations to himself or declaring them only in the presence of intimate friends) may be read as an ironic commentary on this

27

that the separateness is really a unity —

ideology of the incognito as we find it, say, in the writings of Ernst Jünger.

This digression may serve to show, taking an extreme example, what the social implications of such an ontology may be. In the literary field, this particular ideology was of cardinal importance; by destroying the complex tissue of man's relations with his environment, it furthered the dissolution of personality. For it is just the opposition between a man and his environment that determines the development of his personality. There is no great hero of fiction—from Homer's Achilles to Mann's Adrian Leverkühn or Sholochov's Grigory Melyekov—whose personality is not the product of such an opposition. I have shown how disastrous the denial of the distinction between abstract and concrete potentiality must be for the presentation of character. The destruction of the complex tissue of man's interaction with his environment likewise saps the vitality of this opposition. Certainly, some writers who adhere to this ideology have attempted, not unsuccessfully, to portray this opposition in concrete terms. But the underlying ideology deprives these contradictions of their dynamic, developmental significance. The contradictions co-exist, unresolved, contributing to the further dissolution of the personality in question.

It is to the credit of Robert Musil that he was quite conscious of the implications of his method. Of his hero Ulrich he remarked: 'One is faced with a simple choice: either one must run with the pack (when in Rome, do as the Romans do); or one becomes a neurotic.' Musil here introduces the problem, central to all modernist literature, of the significance of psychopathology.

This problem was first widely discussed in the Naturalist period. More than fifty years ago, that doyen of Berlin dramatic critics, Alfred Kerr, was writing: 'Morbidity is the legitimate poetry of Naturalism. For what is poetic in everyday life? Neurotic aberration, escape from life's dreary routine. Only in this way can a character be translated to a rarer clime and yet retain an air of reality.' Interesting, here, is the notion that the

28

poetic necessity of the pathological derives from the prosaic quality of life under capitalism. I would maintain—we shall return to this point—that in modern writing there is a continuity from Naturalism to the Modernism of our day—a continuity restricted, admittedly, to underlying ideological principles. What at first was no more than dim anticipation of approaching catastrophe developed, after 1914, into an all-pervading obsession. And I would suggest that the ever-increasing part played by psychopathology was one of the main features of the continuity. At each period—depending on the prevailing social and historical conditions—psychopathology was given a new emphasis, a different significance and artistic function. Kerr's description suggests that in naturalism the interest in psychopathology sprang from an aesthetic need; it was an attempt to escape from the dreariness of life under capitalism. The quotation from Musil shows that some years later the opposition acquired a moral slant. The obsession with morbidity had ceased to have a merely decorative function, bringing colour into the greyness of reality, and become a moral protest against capitalism.

With Musil—and with many other modernist writers—psychopathology became the goal, the *terminus ad quem,* of their artistic intention. But there is a double difficulty inherent in their intention, which follows from its underlying ideology. There is, first, a lack of definition. The protest expressed by this flight into psychopathology is an abstract gesture; its rejection of reality is wholesale and summary, containing no concrete criticism. It is a gesture, moreover, that is destined to lead nowhere; it is an escape into nothingness. Thus the propagators of this ideology are mistaken in thinking that such a protest could ever be fruitful in literature. In any protest against particular social conditions, these conditions themselves must have the central place. The bourgeois protest against feudal society, the proletarian against bourgeois society, made their point of departure a criticism of the old order. In both cases the protest—reaching out beyond the point of departure—was based on a concrete *terminus ad quem:* the establishment of a new order. How-

29

idea in film — European film reflect an aesthetic expansion to a new order (not polit or social ths) unlike Amer. film that simply reflects, quite effectively, the existing order.

various writers aesthetically — suggesting a direction (an expansion) — or just reflecting, but this later can also be an expansion

ever indefinite the structure and content of this new order, the will towards its more exact definition was not lacking.

How different the protest of writers like Musil! The *terminus a quo* (the corrupt society of our time) is inevitably the main source of energy, since the *terminus ad quem* (the escape into psychopathology) is a mere abstraction. The rejection of modern reality is purely subjective. Considered in terms of man's relation with his environment, it lacks both content and direction. And this lack is exaggerated still further by the character of the *terminus ad quem*. For the protest is an empty gesture, expressing nausea, or discomfort, or longing. Its content—or rather lack of content—derives from the fact that such a view of life cannot impart a sense of direction. These writers are not wholly wrong in believing that psychopathology is their surest refuge; it is the ideological complement of their historical position.

like against Natur Hauptmanns

This obsession with the pathological is not only to be found in literature. Freudian psychoanalysis is its most obvious expression. The treatment of the subject is only superficially different from that in modern literature. As everybody knows, Freud's starting point was 'everyday life'. In order to explain 'slips' and day-dreams, however, he had to have recourse to psychopathology. In his lectures, speaking of resistance and repression, he says: 'Our interest in the general psychology of symptom-formation increases as we understand to what extent the study of pathological conditions can shed light on the workings of the normal mind.' Freud believed he had found the key to the understanding of the normal personality in the psychology of the abnormal. This belief is still more evident in the typology of Kretschmer, which also assumes that psychological abnormalities can explain normal psychology. It is only when we compare Freud's psychology with that of Pavlov, who takes the Hippocratic view that mental abnormality is a deviation from a norm, that we see it in its true light.

dif from Freud?

Clearly, this is not strictly a scientific or literary-critical problem. It is an ideological problem, deriving from the ontological dogma of the solitariness of man. The literature of realism, based on the Aristotelean concept of man as *zoon politikon*, is entitled to develop a new typology for each new phase in the evolution of a society. It displays the contradictions within society and within the individual in the context of a dialectical unity. Here, individuals embodying violent and extraordinary passions are still within the range of a socially normal typology (Shakespeare, Balzac, Stendhal). For, in this literature, the average man is simply a dimmer reflection of the contradictions always existing in man and society; eccentricity is a socially-conditioned distortion. Obviously, the passions of the great heroes must not be confused with 'eccentricity' in the colloquial sense: Christian Buddenbrook is an 'eccentric'; Adrian Leverkühn is not.

The ontology of *Geworfenheit* makes a true typology impossible; it is replaced by an abstract polarity of the eccentric and the socially-average. We have seen why this polarity—which in traditional realism serves to increase our understanding of social normality—leads in modernism to a fascination with morbid eccentricity. Eccentricity becomes the necessary complement of the average; and this polarity is held to exhaust human potentiality. The implications of this ideology are shown in another remark of Musil's: 'If humanity dreamt collectively, it would dream Moosbrugger.' Moosbrugger, you will remember, was a mentally-retarded sexual pervert with homicidal tendencies.

What served, with Musil, as the ideological basis of a new typology—escape into neurosis as a protest against the evils of society—becomes with other modernist writers an immutable *condition humaine*. Musil's statement loses its conditional 'if' and becomes a simple description of reality. Lack of objectivity in the description of the outer world finds its complement in the reduction of reality to a nightmare. Beckett's *Molloy* is perhaps the *ne plus ultra* of this development, although Joyce's vision of reality as an incoherent stream of consciousness had already assumed in Faulkner a nightmare quality. In Beckett's novel we have the same vision twice over. He presents us with an image of the utmost human degradation—an idiot's vegetative existence. Then, as help is imminent from a mysterious unspecified source,

31

the rescuer himself sinks into idiocy. The story is told through the parallel streams of consciousness of the idiot and of his rescuer.

Along with the adoption of perversity and idiocy as types of the *condition humaine*, we find what amounts to frank glorification. Take Montherlant's *Pasiphae*, where sexual perversity— the heroine's infatuation with a bull—is presented as a triumphant return to nature, as the liberation of impulse from the slavery of convention. The chorus—i.e. the author—puts the following question (which, though rhetorical, clearly expects an affirmative reply): 'Si l'absence de pensée et l'absence de morale ne contribuent pas beaucoup à la dignité des bêtes, des plantes et des eaux ... ?' Montherlant expresses as plainly as Musil, though with different moral and emotional emphasis, the hidden —one might say repressed—social character of the protest underlying this obsession with psychopathology, its perverted Rousseauism, its anarchism. There are many illustrations of this in modernist writing. A poem of Benn's will serve to make the point:

> O that we were our primal ancestors,
> Small lumps of plasma in hot, sultry swamps;
> Life, death, conception, parturition
> Emerging from those juices soundlessly.
>
> A frond of seaweed or a dune of sand,
> Formed by the wind and heavy at the base;
> A dragonfly or gull's wing—already, these
> Would signify excessive suffering.

This is not overtly perverse in the manner of Beckett or Montherlant. Yet, in his primitivism, Benn is at one with them. The opposition of man as animal to man as social being (for instance, Heidegger's devaluation of the social as '*das Man*', Klages' assertion of the incompatibility of *Geist* and *Seele*, or Rosenberg's racial mythology) leads straight to a glorification of the abnormal and to an undisguised anti-humanism.

A typology limited in this way to the *homme moyen sensuel* and the idiot also opens the door to 'experimental' stylistic distortion. Distortion becomes as inseparable a part of the portrayal of reality as the recourse to the pathological. But literature must have a concept of the normal if it is to 'place' distortion correctly; that is to say, to see it *as* distortion. With such a typology this placing is impossible, since the normal is no longer a proper object of literary interest. Life under capitalism is, often rightly, presented as a distortion (a petrification or paralysis) of the human substance. But to present psychopathology as a way of escape from this distortion is itself a distortion. We are invited to measure one type of distortion against another and arrive, necessarily, at universal distortion. There is no principle to set against the general pattern, no standard by which the petty-bourgeois and the pathological can be seen in their social context. And these tendencies, far from being relativized with time, become ever more absolute. Distortion becomes the normal condition of human existence; the proper study, the formative principle, of art and literature.

I have demonstrated some of the literary implications of this ideology. Let us now pursue the argument further. It is clear, I think, that modernism must deprive literature of a sense of *perspective*. This would not be surprising; rigorous modernists such as Kafka, Benn, and Musil have always indignantly refused to provide their readers with any such thing. I will return to the ideological implications of the idea of perspective later. Let me say here that, in any work of art, perspective is of overriding importance. It determines the course and content; it draws together the threads of the narration; it enables the artist to choose between the important and the superficial, the crucial and the episodic. The direction in which characters develop is determined by perspective, only those features being described which are material to their development. The more lucid the perspective—as in Molière or the Greeks—the more economical and striking the selection.

Modernism drops this selective principle. It asserts that it can dispense with it, or can replace it with its dogma of the *condition humaine.* A naturalistic style is bound to be the result. This state of affairs—which to my mind characterizes all modernist art of the past fifty years—is disguised by critics who systematically glorify the modernist movement. By concentrating on formal criteria, by isolating technique from content and exaggerating its importance, these critics refrain from judgment on the social or artistic significance of subject-matter. They are unable, in consequence, to make the aesthetic distinction between *realism* and *naturalism.* This distinction depends on the presence or absence in a work of art of a 'hierarchy of significance' in the situations and characters presented. Compared with this, formal categories are of secondary importance. That is why it is possible to speak of the basically *naturalistic* character of modernist literature—and to see here the literary expression of an ideological continuity. This is not to deny that variations in style reflect changes in society. But the particular form this principle of naturalistic arbitrariness, this lack of hierarchic structure, may take is not decisive. We encounter it in the all-determining 'social conditions' of Naturalism, in Symbolism's impressionist methods and its cultivation of the exotic, in the fragmentation of objective reality in Futurism and Constructivism and the German *Neue Sachlichkeit,* or, again, in Surrealism's stream of consciousness.

These schools have in common a basically static approach to reality. This is closely related to their lack of perspective. Characteristically, Gottfried Benn actually incorporated this in his artistic programme. One of his volumes bears the title, *Static Poems.* The denial of history, of development, and thus of perspective, becomes the mark of true insight into the nature of reality.

> The wise man is ignorant
> of change and development
> his children and children's children
> are no part of his world.

34

The rejection of any concept of the future is for Benn the criterion of wisdom. But even those modernist writers who are less extreme in their rejection of history tend to present social and historical phenomena as static. It is, then, of small importance whether this condition is 'eternal', or only a transitional stage punctuated by sudden catastrophes (even in early Naturalism the static presentation was often broken up by these catastrophes, without altering its basic character). Musil, for instance, writes in his essay, *The Writer in our Age*: 'One knows just as little about the present. Partly, this is because we are, as always, too close to the present. But it is also because the present into which we were plunged some two decades ago is of a particularly all-embracing and inescapable character.' Whether or not Musil knew of Heidegger's philosophy, the idea of *Geworfenheit* is clearly at work here. And the following reveals plainly how, for Musil, this static state was upset by the catastrophe of 1914: 'All of a sudden, the world was full of violence. . . . In European civilization, there was a sudden rift. . . .' In short: thus static apprehension of reality in modernist literature is no passing fashion; it is rooted in the ideology of modernism.

To establish the basic distinction between modernism and that realism which, from Homer to Thomas Mann and Gorky, has assumed change and development to be the proper subject of literature, we must go deeper into the underlying ideological problem. In *The House of the Dead* Dostoevsky gave an interesting account of the convict's attitude to work. He described how the prisoners, in spite of brutal discipline, loafed about, working badly or merely going through the motions of work until a new overseer arrived and allotted them a new project, after which they were allowed to go home. 'The work was hard,' Dostoevsky continues, 'but, Christ, with what energy they threw themselves into it! Gone was all their former indolence and pretended incompetence.' Later in the book Dostoevsky sums up his experiences: 'If a man loses hope and has no aim in view, sheer boredom can turn him into a beast. . . .' I have said that the problem of perspective in literature is directly related to the principle of selection. Let me go further: underlying the problem is a pro-found ethical complex, reflected in the composition of the work itself. Every human action is based on a presupposition of its inherent meaningfulness, at least to the subject. Absence of meaning makes a mockery of action and reduces art to naturalistic description.

Clearly, there can be no literature without at least the appear-ance of change or development. This conclusion should not be interpreted in a narrowly metaphysical sense. We have already diagnosed the obsession with psychopathology in modernist literature as a desire to escape from the reality of capitalism. But this implies the absolute primacy of the *terminus a quo*, the condition from which it is desired to escape. Any movement towards a *terminus ad quem* is condemned to impotence. As the ideology of most modernist writers asserts the unalterability of outward reality (even if this is reduced to a mere state of con-sciousness) human activity is, *a priori*, rendered impotent and robbed of meaning.

The apprehension of reality to which this leads is most con-sistently and convincingly realized in the work of Kafka. Kafka remarks of Josef K., as he is being led to execution: 'He thought of flies, their tiny limbs breaking as they struggle away from the fly-paper.' This mood of total impotence, of paralysis in the face of the unintelligible power of circumstances, informs all his work. Though the action of *The Castle* takes a different, even an opposite, direction to that of *The Trial*, this view of the world, from the perspective of a trapped and struggling fly, is all-perva-sive. This experience, this vision of a world dominated by *angst* and of man at the mercy of incomprehensible terrors, makes Kafka's work the very type of modernist art. Techniques, else-where of merely formal significance, are used here to evoke a primitive awe in the presence of an utterly strange and hostile reality. Kafka's *angst* is the experience *par excellence* of modernism.

Two instances from musical criticism—which can afford to be both franker and more theoretical than literary criticism—

36

show that it is indeed a universal experience with which we are dealing. The composer, Hanns Eisler, says of Schönberg: 'Long before the invention of the bomber, he expressed what people were to feel in the air raid shelters.' Even more characteristic—though seen from a modernist point of view—is Theodor W. Adorno's analysis (in *The Ageing of Modern Music*) of symptoms of decadence in modernist music: 'The sounds are still the same. But the experience of *angst*, which made their originals great, has vanished.' Modernist music, he continues, has lost touch with the truth that was its *raison d'être*. Composers are no longer equal to the emotional presuppositions of their modernism. And that is why modernist music has failed. The diminution of the original *angst*-obsessed vision of life (whether due, as Adorno thinks, to inability to respond to the magnitude of the horror or, as I believe, to the fact that this obsession with *angst* among bourgeois intellectuals has already begun to recede) has brought about a loss of substance in modern music, and destroyed its authenticity as a modernist art-form.

This is a shrewd analysis of the paradoxical situation of the modernist artist, particularly where he is trying to express deep and genuine experience. The deeper the experience, the greater the damage to the artistic whole. But this tendency towards disintegration, this loss of artistic unity, cannot be written off as a mere fashion, the product of experimental gimmicks. Modern philosophy, after all, encountered these problems long before modern literature, painting or music. A case in point is the problem of *time*. Subjective Idealism had already separated time, abstractly conceived, from historical change and particularity of place. As if this separation were insufficient for the new age of imperialism, Bergson widened it further. Experienced time, subjective time, now became identical with real time; the rift between this time and that of the objective world was complete. Bergson and other philosophers who took up and varied this theme claimed that their concept of time alone afforded insight into authentic, i.e. subjective, reality. The same tendency soon made its appearance in literature.

The German left-wing critic and essayist of the Twenties, Walter Benjamin, has well described Proust's vision and the techniques he uses to present it in his great novel: 'We all know that Proust does not describe a man's life as it actually happens, but as it is remembered by a man who has lived through it. Yet this puts it far too crudely. For it is not actual experience that is important, but the texture of reminiscence, the Penelope's tapestry of a man's memory.' The connection with Bergson's theories of time is obvious. But whereas with Bergson, in the abstraction of philosophy, the unity of perception is preserved, Benjamin shows that with Proust, as a result of the radical disintegration of the time sequence, objectivity is eliminated: 'A lived event is finite, concluded at least on the level of experience. But a remembered event is infinite, a possible key to everything that preceded it and to everything that will follow it.'

It is the distinction between a philosophical and an artistic vision of the world. However hard philosophy, under the influence of Idealism, tries to liberate the concepts of space and time from temporal and spatial particularity, literature continues to assume their unity. The fact that, nevertheless, the concept of subjective time cropped up in literature only shows how deeply subjectivism is rooted in the experience of the modern bourgeois intellectual. The individual, retreating into himself in despair at the cruelty of the age, may experience an intoxicated fascination with his forlorn condition. But then a new horror breaks through. If reality cannot be understood (or no effort is made to understand it), then the individual's subjectivity—alone in the universe, reflecting only itself—takes on an equally incomprehensible and horrific character. Hugo von Hofmannsthal was to experience this condition very early in his poetic career:

> It is a thing that no man cares to think on,
> And far too terrible for mere complaint,
> That all things slip from us and pass away,
>
> And that my ego, bound by no outward force—
> Once a small child's before it became mine—
> Should now be strange to me, like a strange dog.

By separating time from the outer world of objective reality, the inner world of the subject is transformed into a sinister, inexplicable flux and acquires—paradoxically, as it may seem— a static character.

On literature this tendency towards disintegration, of course, will have an even greater impact than on philosophy. When time is isolated in this way, the artist's world disintegrates into a multiplicity of partial worlds. The static view of the world, now combined with diminished objectivity, here rules unchallenged. The world of man—the only subject-matter of literature—is shattered if a single component is removed. I have shown the consequences of isolating time and reducing it to a subjective category. But time is by no means the only component whose removal can lead to such disintegration. Here, again, Hofmannsthal anticipated later developments. His imaginary 'Lord Chandos' reflects: 'I have lost the ability to concentrate my thoughts or set them out coherently.' The result is a condition of apathy, punctuated by manic fits. The development towards a definitely pathological protest is here anticipated—admittedly in glamorous, romantic guise. But it is the same disintegration that is at work.

Previous realistic literature, however violent its criticism of reality, had always assumed the unity of the world it described and seen it as a living whole inseparable from man himself. But the major realists of our time deliberately introduce elements of disintegration into their work—for instance, the subjectivizing of time—and use them to portray the contemporary world more exactly. In this way, the once natural unity becomes a conscious, constructed unity (I have shown elsewhere that the device of the two temporal planes in Thomas Mann's *Doctor Faustus* serves to emphasize its historicity). But in modernist literature the disintegration of the world of man—and consequently the disintegration of personality—coincides with the ideological intention. Thus *angst*, this basic modern experience, this by-product of *Geworfenheit*, has its emotional origin in the experience of a disintegrating society. But it attains its effects by evoking the disintegration of the world of man.

To complete our examination of modernist literature, we must consider for a moment the question of allegory. Allegory is that aesthetic genre which lends itself par excellence to a description of man's alienation from objective reality. Allegory is a problematic genre because it rejects that assumption of an immanent meaning to human existence which—however unconscious, however combined with religious concepts of transcendence—is the basis of traditional art. Thus in medieval art we observe a new secularity (in spite of the continued use of religious subjects) triumphing more and more, from the time of Giotto, over the allegorizing of an earlier period.

Certain reservations should be made at this point. First, we must distinguish between literature and the visual arts. In the latter, the limitations of allegory can be the more easily overcome in that transcendental, allegorical subjects can be clothed in an aesthetic immanence (even if of a merely decorative kind) and the rift in reality in some sense be eliminated—we have only to think of Byzantine mosaic art. This decorative element has no real equivalent in literature; it exists only in a figurative sense, and then only as a secondary component. Allegorical art of the quality of Byzantine mosaic is only rarely possible in literature. Secondly, we must bear in mind in examining allegory—and this is of great importance for our argument—a historical distinction: does the concept of transcendence in question contain within itself tendencies towards immanence (as in Byzantine art or Giotto), or is it the product precisely of a rejection of these tendencies?

Allegory, in modernist literature, is clearly of the latter kind. Transcendence implies here, more or less consciously, the negation of any meaning immanent in the world or the life of man. We have already examined the underlying ideological basis of this view and its stylistic consequences. To conclude our analysis, and to establish the allegorical character of modernist literature, I must refer again to the work of one of the finest theoreticians of modernism—to Walter Benjamin. Benjamin's examination of allegory was a product of his researches into German Baroque drama. Benjamin made his analysis of these relatively minor plays the occasion for a general discussion of the aesthetics of allegory. He was asking, in effect, why it is that transcendence, which is the essence of allegory, cannot but destroy aesthetics itself.

Benjamin gives a very contemporary definition of allegory. He does not labour the analogies between modern art and the Baroque (such analogies are tenuous at best, and were much overdone by the fashionable criticism of the time). Rather, he uses the Baroque drama to criticize modernism, imputing the characteristics of the latter to the former. In so doing, Benjamin became the first critic to attempt a philosophical analysis of the aesthetic paradox underlying modernist art. He writes:

> In Allegory, the *facies hippocratica* of history looks to the observer like a petrified primeval landscape. History, all the suffering and failure it contains, finds expression in the human face—or, rather, in the human skull. No sense of freedom, no classical proportion, no human emotion lives in its features—not only human existence in general, but the fate of every individual human being is symbolized in this most palpable token of mortality. This is the core of the allegorical vision, of the Baroque idea of history as the passion of the world; History is significant only in the stations of its corruption. Significance is a function of mortality—because it is death that marks the passage from corruptibility to meaningfulness. *(doesn't meaningfulness imply eternity?)*

Benjamin returns again and again to this link between allegory and the annihilation of history:

> In the light of this vision history appears, not as the gradual realization of the eternal, but as a process of inevitable decay. Allegory thus goes beyond beauty. What ruins are in the physical world, allegories are in the world of the mind.

Benjamin points here to the aesthetic consequences of modernism —though projected into the Baroque drama—more shrewdly and consistently than any of his contemporaries. He sees that the notion of objective time is essential to any understanding of history, and that the notion of subjective time is a product of a period of decline. 'A thorough knowledge of the problematic nature of art' thus becomes for him—correctly, from his point of view—one of the hall-marks of allegory in Baroque drama. It is problematic, on the one hand, because it is an art intent on expressing absolute transcendence that fails to do so because of the means at its disposal. It is also problematic because it is an art reflecting the corruption of the world and bringing about its own dissolution in the process. Benjamin discovers 'an immense, anti-aesthetic subjectivity' in Baroque literature, associated with 'a theologically-determined subjectivity'. (We shall presently show—a point I have discussed elsewhere in relation to Heidegger's philosophy—how in literature a 'religious atheism' of this kind can acquire a theological character.) Romantic—and, on a higher plane, Baroque—writers were well aware of this problem, and gave their understanding, not only theoretical, but artistic—that is to say allegorical—expression. 'The image,' Benjamin remarks, 'becomes a rune in the sphere of allegorical intuition. When touched by the light of theology, its symbolic beauty is gone. The false appearance of totality vanishes. The image dies; the parable no longer holds true: the world it once contained disappears.'

The consequences for art are far-reaching, and Benjamin does not hesitate to point them out: 'Every person, every object, every relationship can stand for something else. This transferability constitutes a devastating, though just, judgment on the profane world—which is thereby branded as a world where such things are of small importance.' Benjamin knows, of course, that although details are 'transferable', and thus insignificant, they are not banished from art altogether. On the contrary. Precisely in modern art, with which he is ultimately concerned, descriptive detail is often of an extraordinary sensuous, suggestive power—we think again of Kafka. But this, as we showed in the case of Musil (a writer who does not consciously aim at allegory) does

42

not prevent the materiality of the world from undergoing permanent alteration, from becoming transferable and arbitrary. Just this, modernist writers maintain, is typical of their own apprehension of reality. Yet presented in this way, the world becomes, as Benjamin puts it, 'exalted and depreciated at the same time'. For the conviction that phenomena are *not* ultimately transferable is rooted in a belief in the world's rationality and in man's ability to penetrate its secrets. In realistic literature each descriptive detail is both *individual* and *typical*. Modern allegory, and modernist ideology, however, deny the *typical*. By destroying the coherence of the world, they reduce detail to the level of mere particularity (once again, the connection between modernism and naturalism is plain). Detail, in its allegorical transferability, though brought into a direct, if paradoxical connection with transcendence, becomes an abstract function of the transcendence to which it points. Modernist literature thus replaces concrete typicality with abstract particularity.

We are here applying Benjamin's paradox directly to aesthetics and criticism, and particularly to the aesthetics of modernism. And, though we have reversed his scale of values, we have not deviated from the course of his argument. Elsewhere, he speaks out even more plainly—as though the Baroque mask had fallen, revealing the modernist skull underneath:

> Allegory is left empty-handed. The forces of evil, lurking in its depths, owe their very existence to allegory. Evil is, precisely, the non-existence of that which allegory purports to represent.

The paradox Benjamin arrives at—his investigation of the aesthetics of Baroque tragedy has culminated in a negation of aesthetics—sheds a good deal of light on modernist literature, and particularly on Kafka. In interpreting his writings allegorically I am not, of course, following Max Brod, who finds a specifically religious allegory in Kafka's works. Kafka refuted any such interpretation in a remark he is said to have made to Brod himself: 'We are nihilistic figments, all of us; suicidal notions forming in God's mind.' Kafka rejected, too, the gnostic concept of

43

God as an evil demiurge: 'The world is a cruel whim of God, an evil day's work.' When Brod attempted to give this an optimistic slant, Kafka shrugged off the attempt ironically: 'Oh, hope enough, hope without end—but not, alas, for us.' These remarks, quoted by Benjamin in his brilliant essay on Kafka, point to the general spiritual climate of his work: 'His profoundest experience is of the hopelessness, the utter meaninglessness of man's world, and particularly that of present-day bourgeois man.' Kafka, whether he says so openly or not, is an atheist. An atheist, though, of that modern species who regard God's removal from the scene not as a liberation—as did Epicurus and the Encyclopedists—but as a token of the 'God-forsakenness' of the world, its utter desolation and futility. Jacobsen's *Niels Lyhne* was the first novel to describe this state of mind of the atheistic bourgeois intelligentsia. Modern religious atheism is characterized, on the one hand, by the fact that unbelief has lost its revolutionary *élan*—the empty heavens are the projection of a world beyond hope of redemption. On the other hand, religious atheism shows that the desire for salvation lives on with undiminished force in a world without God, worshipping the void created by God's absence.

The supreme judges in *The Trial*, the castle administration in *The Castle*, represent transcendence in Kafka's allegories: the transcendence of Nothingness. Everything points to them, and they could give meaning to everything. Everybody believes in their existence and omnipotence; but nobody knows them, nobody knows how they can be reached. If there is a God here, it can only be the God of religious atheism: *atheos absconditus*. We become acquainted with a repellent host of subordinate authorities; brutal, corrupt, pedantic—and, at the same time, unreliable and irresponsible. It is a portrait of the bourgeois society Kafka knew, with a dash of Prague local colouring. But it is also allegorical in that the doings of this bureaucracy and of those dependent on it, its impotent victims, are not concrete and realistic, but a reflection of that Nothingness which governs existence. The hidden, non-existent God of Kafka's world derives his spectral character from the fact that his own non-existence is the ground of all existence; and the portrayed reality, uncannily accurate as it is, is spectral in the shadow of that dependence. The only purpose of transcendence—the intangible *nichtendes Nichts*—is to reveal the *facies hippocratica* of the world.

That abstract particularity which we saw to be the aesthetic consequence of allegory reaches its high mark in Kafka. He is a marvellous observer; the spectral character of reality affects him so deeply that the simplest episodes have an oppressive, nightmarish immediacy. As an artist, he is not content to evoke the surface of life. He is aware that individual detail must point to general significance. But how does he go about the business of abstraction? He has emptied everyday life of meaning by using the allegorical method; he has allowed detail to be annihilated by his transcendental Nothingness. This allegorical transcendence bars Kafka's way to realism, prevents him from investing observed detail with typical significance. Kafka is not able, in spite of his extraordinary evocative power, in spite of his unique sensibility, to achieve that fusion of the particular and the general which is the essence of realistic art. His aim is to raise the individual detail in its immediate particularity (without generalizing its content) to the level of abstraction. Kafka's method is typical, here, of modernism's allegorical approach. Specific subject-matter and stylistic variation do not matter; what matters is the basic ideological determination of form and content. The particularity we find in Beckett and Joyce, in Musil and Benn, various as the treatment of it may be, is essentially of the same kind.

If we combine what we have up to now discussed separately we arrive at a consistent pattern. We see that modernism leads not only to the destruction of traditional literary forms; it leads to the destruction of literature as such. And this is true not only of Joyce, or of the literature of Expressionism and Surrealism. It was not André Gide's ambition, for instance, to bring about a revolution in literary style; it was his philosophy that compelled him to abandon conventional forms. He planned his *Faux-*

Monnayeurs as a novel. But its structure suffered from a characteristically modernist schizophrenia: it was supposed to be written by the man who was also the hero of the novel. And, in practice, Gide was forced to admit that no novel, no work of literature could be constructed in that way. We have here a practical demonstration that—as Benjamin showed in another context—modernism means not the enrichment, but the negation of art.

Franz Kafka or Thomas Mann?

To DEFINE the conditions in which bourgeois 'literary' literature can flourish today, we analysed the ideological basis and the main stylistic tendencies of the modern bourgeois anti-realistic movement. We might have widened our examination to include 'non-literary' literature, if only to reveal its social basis. Certain of the phenomena we have discussed are to be found most strikingly in this latter literature. Take the cult of the abnormal, of the perverse: horror comics show that this cult is drawn directly from life. Or take the detective story. With Conan Doyle the genre was firmly grounded in a philosophy of security; it glorified the omniscience of those who watched over the stability of bourgeois life. Now the basic ingredients are fear and insecurity: at any moment terror may break through; only luck can avert it. In some works of a middle-brow kind (for example in Hayes' *On a day like any other*) this kind of 'luck' provides—by way of apology for the society it portrays—the book's happy ending. Indeed, a main distinction between high-brow literature and the literature of entertainment is just this rejection of a compromise—though there is a modern variety of the thriller which deliberately exploits horror for its own purposes.

But we must return to our proper subject: to modernism, or rather to those modernist techniques so influential on the contemporary literary scene. We avoided the use of purely formal criteria in distinguishing between modernist and realist literature. Yet ideological criteria, though they underlie and mould literary expression, also represent no more than general tendencies. These may co-exist in one author, even in one work of art, with varying degrees of emphasis and self-consciousness.

Indeed, if we refuse to follow those modernist critics who tell us that theirs is the only possible future literature, and trace the realist tendencies still existing within the anti-realistic movement, the literature of our time begins to resemble an extended battlefield. It is a battlefield where the champions of modern anti-realism, and the champions of what we have called 'the revolt of humanism', noisily contend. What we are examining is not simply two typical literary movements of our time. We are examining a conflict between two basic tendencies, a conflict fought out, not only in one and the same writer, but often in one and the same poem, play, or novel.

The dividing line is often blurred, if only because all writing must contain a certain degree of realism. Indeed, there is a fundamental truth at stake here: realism is not one style among others, it is the basis of literature; all styles (even those seemingly most opposed to realism) originate in it or are significantly related to it. Schopenhauer's remark that a consistent solipsist could only be found in a lunatic asylum is applicable to consistent anti-realism. The inevitability of realism is most obvious, of course, where descriptive detail is concerned. We have only to think of Kafka, where the most improbable, fantastic statements appear real through force of descriptive detail. Without this realism in detail Kafka's evocation of the spectral nature of human existence would be no more than a sermon, not the inexorable nightmare it is. Realistic detail is a precondition for the communication of a sense of absurdity. We get, in fact, not straightforward anti-realism, but a dialectical process in which realism of detail negates the reality described; everything is determined by it—the presentation, the structure, the coherence of the writing. Similar processes are at work elsewhere in other modernist literature. But the tension Kafka achieves by pushing his two poles to their extremes, and by the shock of his transitions, is lacking. In Musil, too, we find this tension, but it owes less to intensity of detail and is spread out over the whole extent of his novel. We encounter dialectical leaps from 'documentary' (with regard to some of the characters the novel is a *roman à clef*) to intimations of timelessness—attempts to achieve that 'ahistoric', 'paradigmatic' ambience which Musil claimed for the work.

Of still greater importance is the fact that many—and not the least extreme—components of modernist literature (for instance, the problem of time) are not as far removed from contemporary life as it might seem. On the contrary, they reflect very well certain aspects of reality, certain contemporary characteristics and peculiarities (of a certain social class, at least). Even with the most abstruse anti-realistic writers, stylistic experiment is not the wilful twisting of reality according to subjective whim: it is a consequence of conditions prevailing in the modern world. Modernist forms, like other literary forms, reflect social and historical realities—though in a distorted, and distorting, fashion.

The situation is immensely complicated; it is natural that in the private statements and public manifestoes of leading modernist writers the issues are often blurred. It is not enough to point to the protests against the suppression of 'degenerate art' under Hitler. These protests proclaimed general freedom of literary expression, but they defended more specifically the writer's duty to describe reality as his artistic conscience dictates. Since truth was the enemy of Hitlerism, a protest against its persecution of 'degenerate art' was at the same time a defence of realism.

The motives of the modernists' opposition to Stalinist dogmatism's rejection of 'formalism' are likewise mixed. Defence of extreme modernism (including genuinely 'formalistic' literature) goes hand in hand with a—justified—rejection of the dogmatists' over-simplifications about the subject-matter and style of realism, and of their tendency to suppress the contradictions existing in socialist society, their reduction of 'socialist perspective' to childish 'happy endings'.

Attacks of this kind may cause the pendulum to swing to the other extreme. Seeing that dogmatism paralyses originality, the modernist critic is tempted to contrast—an understandable, though objectively incorrect reaction—the 'interesting' colourfulness of decadent art with the 'greyness' of schematic social-realist pseudo-literature. In the process he is likely to dismiss the theory of socialist realism as an obstacle to artistic freedom. The significant aesthetic antagonism between realism and anti-realism is no longer considered worth discussing; the merits of socialist (and critical) realism are disregarded; and the deeply problematical nature of modernism itself is ignored. In this context, it is worth pointing out the schematism of so many of the most highly praised creations of modernism. Formal novelty, and an affected originality, often conceal a subjectivist dogmatism. Ernst Jünger and Gottfried Benn, James Joyce and Samuel Beckett are not, properly speaking, a whit less schematic than many social-realist writers.

More significant than such polemics—where often enough the adversary, rather than the object to be defended, seems to determine the course of the argument—are the utterances of those critical realists who had an interest in, and concern for, the formal experimentation of modernism, and expressed the conviction that they had many basic attitudes in common. The reason is not far to seek. Many of these experiments are, in effect, reflections of contemporary reality. If realistic writers sympathize with these experiments, and are stimulated thereby to widen the scope of realism, it is because they wish to find new means to deal with contemporary subject-matter. We have only to think of Thomas Mann's published opinions of Kafka, Joyce, or Gide.

However blurred in a particular work of art, these distinctions exist; and can often be traced in individual cases with some precision. They are, indeed, more than bare distinctions; they are often mutually exclusive contradictions. We have already pointed to examples of polarization of content and, as a consequence, of form in cases that appear superficially similar—the handling of the stream-of-consciousness technique in Joyce and Thomas Mann, and the apparently similar, though in fact diametrically opposed, treatment of time. And there is a reason for this outward convergence in spite of extreme inner divergence. While the modernist writer is uncritical towards many aspects of the modern world, his contemporary, the realist writer, can step

50

back from these things and treat them with the necessary critical
detachment. To take the problem of time: Thomas Mann's critical detachment is such that he is not in doubt about the subjective character of the modern experience of time. Yet he knows *Proust?*
that this experience is typical only of a certain social class, which
can best be portrayed by making use of this experience. The uncritical approach of modernist writers—and of some modern
philosophers—reveals itself in their conviction that this subjective experience constitutes reality as such. That is why this treatment of time can be used by the realistic writer to characterize
certain figures in his novels, although in a modernist work it may
be used to describe reality itself. Again and again Thomas Mann
places characters with a time-experience of this subjectivist kind
in relation to characters whose experience of time is normal and
objective. In *The Magic Mountain* Hans Castorp represents the
former type; Joachim Ziemssen and Hofrat Behrens the latter.
Ziemssen is aware that this experience of time may be a result of
living in a sanatorium, hermetically sealed off from everyday life.
We arrive, therefore, at an important distinction: the modernist
writer identifies what is necessarily a subjective experience with
reality as such, thus giving a distorted picture of reality as a
whole (Virginia Woolf is an extreme example of this). The realist, with his critical detachment, places what is a significant,
specifically modern experience in a wider context, giving
it only the emphasis it deserves as part of a greater, objective
whole.

The same distinction is valid with regard to descriptive detail.
In isolation, descriptive detail may be a genuine enough reflection of reality—that is, if the writer in question has talent. But
whether or not the sequence and organization make for an
adequate image of objective reality will depend on the writer's
attitude towards reality as a whole. For this attitude determines
the function which the individual detail is accorded in the context of the whole. If it is handled uncritically, the result may be
an arbitrary naturalism, since the writer will not be able to
distinguish between significant and irrelevant detail. Joyce, I

think, is a case in point. Once again, the essentially naturalistic character of modernism comes to the fore.

The matter becomes more complex with Kafka. Kafka is one of the very few modernist writers whose attitude to detail is selective, not naturalistic. Formally, his treatment of detail is not dissimilar to that of a realist. The difference becomes apparent only when we examine his basic commitment, the principles determining the selection and sequence of detail. With Kafka these principles are his belief in a transcendental force (Nothingness); in his nihilistic allegories, therefore, the artistic unity is broken.

But the problem cannot be approached formalistically. There are great realistic writers in whose work immediate social and historical reality is transcended, where realism in detail is based on a belief in a supernatural world. Take E. T. A. Hoffmann, for example. In Hoffmann, realism in detail goes hand in hand with a belief in the spectral nature of reality. On closer inspection, though, the difference between his artistic aims and those of modernism is apparent. Hoffmann's world is—for all its fairy-tale, ghostly ambience—an accurate enough reflection of conditions in the Germany of his time, a country moving from a distorted feudal absolutism to a capitalism not less distorted. With Hoffmann the supernatural was a means of presenting the German situation in its totality, at a time when social conditions did not as yet allow a direct realistic description or, indeed, as yet reveal a typical pattern. The working out of a typology was much easier in more highly developed France—though even Balzac at times used methods developed by Hoffmann (*Melmoth Reconcilié*).

Kafka is more secular than Hoffmann. His ghosts belong to everyday bourgeois life; and, since this life itself is unreal, there is no need of supernatural ghosts à la Hoffmann. But the unity of the world is broken up, since an essentially subjective vision is identified with reality itself. The terror generated by the world of imperialist capitalism (anticipatory of its later fascist progeny), where human beings are degraded to mere objects—this fear, originally a subjective experience, becomes an objective entity.

The reflection of a distortion becomes a distorted reflection. And though Kafka's artistic method differs from that of other modernist writers, the principle of presentation is the same: the world is an allegory of transcendent Nothingness. With Kafka's followers the differences grow smaller or disappear altogether. With Beckett, for example, who mixes Kafkaesque and Joycean motifs, a fully standardized nihilistic modernism is the end-product.

In rejecting a rigid distinction, and acknowledging that in many cases the distinction is blurred, I must not be taken to imply that no real opposition exists. On the contrary, only by this method can the conflict of tendencies be accurately assessed. To sum up our enquiry so far: similarity of technique does not imply similarity of ideology; nor is the approval or rejection of certain techniques a pointer to a writer's basic aim.

But what is this basic aim? So far, we have dealt with the main components of modernism, tracing the central ideological position common to its various schools. In order to establish our distinction we must return to the question of *perspective*. First, we must show how perspective acts as a principle of selection, as the criterion by which a writer selects his detail and avoids the pitfalls of naturalism. Clearly, this problem faces every talented writer: literary talent implies an affection for the richness and diversity of life. How the individual writer imposes some kind of order on the profusion of sensuous impression is chiefly a biographical question. These two dialectically opposed, yet dialectically complementary, activities are basic to the formation of an individual style. And here the importance of perspective as the selective principle must be evident. Max Liebermann, the Berlin Impressionist, used to say: 'To draw is to subtract.' We might extend that aphorism: art is the selection of the essential and subtraction of the inessential.

In itself, this is too abstract a definition. If it is to be of practical use, we must enquire more deeply into the subjective principle guiding artistic selection, and investigate the convergence (or divergence) between the data selected by an individual writer and 'artistic objectivity'. The latter is clearly not a direct consequence of the former; the degree of sincerity, intensity and insight guiding artistic selection is no guarantee, let alone a criterion, of objectivity. Yet it would be wrong to see the two principles as ineluctably opposed. Certainly, there is a divergence between subjective aim and objective achievement. But it is not something abrupt and irrational, a distinction between two metaphysical entities. Rather, it is part of the dialectical process by which a creative subjectivity develops, and is expressive of that subjectivity's encounter with the world of its time (or, possibly, of its failure to come to terms with that world).

A writer's pattern of choice is a function of his personality. But personality is not in fact timeless and absolute, however it may appear to the individual consciousness. Talent and character may be innate; but the manner in which they develop, or fail to develop, depends on the writer's interaction with his environment, on his relationships with other human beings. His life is part of the life of his time; no matter whether he is conscious of this, approves of it or disapproves. He is part of a larger social and historical whole.

His own life is thus never constant or static; it is a process, a running battle between past, present and future. It is something which cannot be measured or understood until its stages have been experienced as a movement from and towards a certain goal. These stages and their dynamic interrelations are not purely subjective elements, to be accepted or rejected by the writer at his discretion. Life itself, the categories determining its nature and development, would be distorted if such factors were to be arbitrarily eliminated.

Up to this point, and within the framework of this rather abstract philosophical analysis, I may have the reader's approval. But a historical phenomenon is historical not only in this general sense; it is also a *concrete* element in a specific historical process, in a concrete present linking a concrete past and future. It follows that everything in a writer's life, every individual experience, thought and emotion he undergoes, however subjective, partakes of a historical character. Every element in his life as a

54

human being and as a writer is part of, and determined by, the movement from and towards some goal. Any authentic reflection of reality in literature must point to this movement. The method adopted will vary, of course, with the period and personality. But the selection and subtraction he undertakes in response to the teleological pattern of his own life constitutes the most intimate link between a writer's subjectivity and the outside world. We observe here a dialectical leap from the profound inwardness of subjectivity to the objectivity of social and historical reality.

In all this, *perspective* plays a decisive role. To understand its importance we must go into the distinction between objective reality and its artistic reflection rather more fully. It is a truism that the roots of the present are in the past, and the roots of the future in the present. Objectively, perspective points to the main movements in a given historical process. Subjectively—and not only in the field of artistic activity—it represents the capacity to grasp the existence and mode of action of these movements. If literature is to render an image of life that is adequate, formally convincing and consistent, the sequence must be reversed. Whereas in life 'whither?' is a consequence of 'whence?', in literature 'whither?' determines the content, selection and proportion of the various elements. The finished work may resemble life in observing a causal sequence; but it would be no more than an arbitrary chronicle if there were not this reversal of direction. It is the perspective, the *terminus ad quem*, that determines the significance of each element in a work of art.

The creative role of perspective goes even further than this and touches on the creative act itself. It is not enough, however, to demonstrate the general connection between perspective and literary creativity. The concreteness of a writer's perspective, of course, is a decisive influence on the vitality and suggestive power of his art. It is decisive in as much as there is a connection—not direct, but complex and devious—between the structure of individual character and the degree to which perspective, in a work of art, can be realized. An *aesthetic* explanation of this connection has never been attempted; nor, I think, has the question ever been posed. In this place, we can do no more than enquire into one or two extreme examples. And this only in relation to our specific problem—to discover what perspective is favourable to the development of critical realism at the present day.

The following points seem to me worth making. First, there exists a somewhat abstract perspective, which makes use of the general features of an historical period, and can be employed in satire to work out typical characters and situations (Swift, Saltykov-Shchedrin). Clearly, typical situations will be technically easier to realize than characters which are individual and typical at the same time. Secondly, at the opposite extreme, there is the kind of perspective mainly concerned with day-to-day depiction of events, and which encourages the naturalistic description of individual or superficially typical features. The dialectic of historical development is labyrinthine; and, especially in regard to individual particularities, is not open to detached contemporary prediction. Only 'prophetic' vision, or subsequent study of a completed period, can grasp the unity underlying sharp contradictions. One would be misunderstanding the role of perspective in literature, though, if one were to identify 'prophetic' understanding with correct political foresight. If such foresight were the criterion, there would have been no successful typology in nineteenth-century literature. For it was precisely the greatest writers of that age—Balzac and Stendhal, Dickens and Tolstoy— who erred most in their view of what the future would be like. Yet it was not accident that made possible the creation of typical, universal characters in their work.

Typology and perspective are thus related in a special way. The great realist writer is alone able to grasp and portray trends and phenomena truthfully in their historical development— 'trends' not so much in the social and political field, as in that area where human behaviour is moulded and evaluated, where existing types are developed further and new types emerge. Men are changed by forces in their environment. But it is not only the character of individual human beings that changes. Greater emphasis is given at certain times to certain specific problems: some are pushed into the foreground, others eliminated; certain characteristics acquire a tragic aura, others, tragic in the past, are now reduced to comic dimensions. Such shifts of emphasis go on perpetually throughout history. Yet only the greatest realists are equipped to understand and portray their complexity.

A writer may grasp the authentic human problem (and thus the authentic social problem) of a particular phase in the historical process without consciously anticipating subsequent political and social developments. Here again, the question of perspective is relevant. For a typology can only be of lasting significance if the writer has depicted the central or peripheral significance, the comic or tragic characteristics of his types, in such a way that subsequent developments confirm his portrait of the age. (Balzac and Tolstoy have this kind of lasting significance; Ibsen, by way of contrast, has dated in many respects). We see now that perspective is not to be confused with the capacity to predict historical events. Yet we also see why a perspective that sticks too closely to day-to-day events is rarely successful: concrete and determinate in matters which are of small interest to literature, it fails to produce adequate aesthetic solutions in more important matters. Lasting typologies, based on a perspective of this sort, owe their effectiveness not to the artist's understanding of day-to-day events, but to his unconscious possession of a perspective independent of, and reaching beyond, his understanding of the contemporary scene.

Perspective, in this concrete form, is central to our problem. For there is an intimate connection between a writer's ability to create lasting human types (the real criterion of literary achievement) and his allegiance to an ideology which allows of a belief in social development. Any attempt to substitute a static immobilism for the dynamic movement of history must reduce the significance, the universality, of the typology in question. Even in the Naturalist period the difficulty of creating living characters had increased so much that a writer of Zola's stature could not create one really memorable character. The

57

state of affairs in modernist literature is still more striking. It takes, of course, a different form with each individual writer. But we are less interested in the particular form the reduction takes— whether the reduction of character to shadowy blur, or a submission to a rigid and superficial stylization, or a surrender to mystical irrationalism. Equally, there will be modernist theoreticians who refuse to admit that this reduction is anything negative. They will claim for Beckett's characters the dignity of a new typology, or reject the whole business of type-creation as a hangover from the nineteenth century.

It may be useful here to listen to the views of certain writers whose approach is not ideological and philosophical, but who are guided rather by practical experience of their craft. In a different context, some years ago, I quoted a remark of Sinclair Lewis' about John Dos Passos. Lewis praised Dos Passos' 'natural'—i.e. modernist—compositional methods as an enormous advance on older narrative conventions. Yet, speaking of the creation of character, he was forced to conclude: 'It is undeniable that Dos Passos has failed so far to produce characters as memorable as Pickwick, Micawber, Oliver Twist or David Copperfield or Nicholas Nickleby ... and he will probably never do so.'

No less interesting is a confession of Camus's in his preface to the writings of Roger Martin du Gard. Martin du Gard's characters, Camus remarks, display a density, a three-dimensionality, very unusual in contemporary literature. The significant literature of our time, he continues, goes back to Dostoevsky rather than to Tolstoy. Its heroes are passionate, gesticulating shadows meditating upon human fate. Camus brilliantly contrasts Dostoevsky's young women in *The Possessed* with Tolstoy's Natasha Rostova: 'The distinction is like that between a film and stage character: the presence is spiritual, incorporeal.' I have no space here to comment on Camus's illuminating discussion of Dostoevsky and Kafka. The contrast between the two artistic modes is worked out with remarkable impartiality. Camus does not omit to point out that Dostoevsky's art is infinitely richer than that of his followers, who often inherit little more than the shadowiness to which he reduces human personality.

This judgment is the more interesting as we find in Camus's own work a comparable reduction of human personality. For, however suggestive as an allegory of the *condition humaine*, and however subtle the moral problems thrown up by Camus's description of the plague, the characters in *La Peste* remain, by Camus's definition, shadows. Yet it is not the spare style, maintained with marvellous consistency, which has brought about this reduction; it is the lack of perspective. The lives of his characters are without direction, without motivation, without development. Camus's plague—the choice of subject-matter is characteristic—is not shown as an accidental disaster, as a horrific interlude in the continuity of human life. The plague is the reality of human existence itself, the terror of which has no beginning and no end. Camus's admiration for Roger Martin du Gard's typology is significant, because it contains a profound, though unstated, criticism of his own work.

These apparent digressions may, I hope, have served to shed some light on the role of perspective in literature. We must now take a further, decisive step in the argument—with the proposition that no writer of the past century, asking himself to what goal history is moving, has been able to ignore socialism.

The writers of the 'humanist revolt', and their contemporaries, had to face this challenge. It was Zola who said that whenever he set out to tackle a new problem he always came up against socialism. Again, it is significant for Gerhart Hauptmann's artistic development—and for the enormous impact of his early Naturalist work—that the problem of socialism, though vaguely articulated, was always present in his mind. Once this vision lost its validity for him, Hauptmann plunged into that prolonged creative crisis which caused his admirers to fear for his future as a writer. There is no lack of other examples: the decisive role played by socialism in the work of Anatole France, of Romain Rolland, of George Bernard Shaw, is sufficiently well-known. And Roger Martin du Gard's criticism of bourgeois society, in his cycle of novels, is no less determined by a *terminus ad quem* of this kind—Jacques Thibault's encounter with socialism.

A simple conclusion would appear to be available at this point. Is not the decisive distinction that between the presence of a socialist perspective in socialist realism, and its absence in decadent bourgeois literature?

The conclusion is tempting, but false. For the distinction I have in mind, the ideological and artistic implications of which I am concerned to analyse, is operative within bourgeois literature itself. The true opposition is not between socialist realism and bourgeois modernism, but between bourgeois critical realism and bourgeois modernism. Not everyone who looks for a solution to the social and ideological crisis of bourgeois society—and this is necessarily the subject-matter of contemporary bourgeois literature—will be a professed socialist. It is enough that a writer takes socialism into account and does not reject it out of hand. But if he rejects socialism—and this is the point I want to make —he closes his eyes to the future, gives up any chance of assessing the present correctly, and loses the ability to create other than purely static works of art.

Ideologically, this question has been central to bourgeois literature throughout the past century; indeed, it has become increasingly urgent. Let us look at some of its earlier appearances. A hundred years ago Heine wrote in a preface to the French edition of *Lutezia* that communism, though it was against his interests and his natural inclinations, had an attraction he found hard to resist. One reason for this attraction was communism's emphasis on logic and on justice. The unjust society he lived in stood condemned—even though the new society, as he put it, should use his *Buch der Lieder* as 'wrapping paper for an old lady's coffee'. Another reason was as cogent, if Machiavellian: the communists were the most powerful enemies of his own old enemy, German reaction and German chauvinism. In spite of all this, Heine never became a socialist. But he did take up a position towards socialism which enabled him to look at the bourgeois society of his day, and at the future, without illusions.

Let us look at the changing forms perspective has taken for the bourgeois writer over the course of history. Before the French Revolution, realism did not have to face this problem. Perspective went no further than the overthrow of the feudal society of absolutism. The shape of the new bourgeois society was—from the point of view of the artist—of secondary importance. This was to change after the French Revolution. The degree to which the works of Goethe and Balzac, of Stendhal and Tolstoy, are still interlarded with utopian elements is very striking. It expresses their ambiguity towards bourgeois society. On the one hand, we still find a bourgeois-progressive perspective (with Tolstoy, it is still peasant-plebeian) which is rooted in, and does not look beyond, bourgeois society. But on the other hand there is a deeply felt need to go beyond the mere affirmation of existing conditions, to explore values not to be found in present society—values which come to be thought of, necessarily, as hidden in the future. Thus the utopian perspective serves a double function: it enables the artist to portray the present age truthfully without giving way to despair.

A later phase of critical realism—Flaubert is a good example—rejects such utopianism with a gesture of ascetic defiance. Utopian writing in this period takes the form of an escape into exoticisms whether of time or place. This dual critique—ironic detachment from his own ineradicable romanticism, but also rejection of a bourgeois world condemned by the standards of that romanticism—enabled Flaubert to view his age without hope, but also without fear. In bourgeois realism his is a strange borderline case: Flaubert's portrayal of society hints occasionally at the coming dichotomy, but it preserves much of the richness and truth-to-life of earlier realism. After Flaubert, new problems come to the fore. But, before entering into these, it may be useful to instance the tendencies running counter to realism in the literature of the age.

At the time when Heine was composing his later works—about a decade after the above confession—another writer put down his views on the subject—Dostoevsky, in his story *From the Darkness of the City*. This story contains perhaps the first authentic description of the isolation of modern bourgeois man—an interesting ideological link between Dostoevsky and modernism. Yet Dostoevsky still sees such isolation in a social context. He does not idealize it; rather, he paints it in a pessimistic hue and shows it to be a blind alley. The social circumstances and consequences of this isolation are clearly seen by Dostoevsky—where modernism would tend to mystify. His hero's sufferings derive from the inhumanity of early capitalism, and particularly from its destructive influence on personal relationships. Dostoevsky loathes capitalism with all his being; but he rejects a socialist solution no less passionately. His protest against the inhumanity of capitalism is transformed into a sophistical, anti-capitalist romanticism, into a critique of socialism and democracy. Thus, fear of socialism completes the isolation of man in capitalist society (though with Dostoevsky this isolation is to some extent concealed by his pan-Slav clerical mysticism).

Dostoevsky represents, of course, a comparatively early stage in this evolution. Nietzsche, who substitutes a critique of bourgeois philistinism for this critique of bourgeois inhumanity, generalizes the attitude towards life described in Dostoevsky's story, *The Cellar*. This is not the place to show how Nietzsche's identification of capitalism and socialism, his raising of the spectre of 'mass culture', his rejection of democracy and progress, helped to prepare the way for Hitler's demagogy. I attempted this in my book, *The Destruction of Reason*. There, I tried to show how these tendencies had lived on in a modified form after Hitler's defeat. The opposition to socialism gathered momentum and was soon transformed into an ideological crusade which, though nominally concerned with the preservation of democracy, was really nourished by a growing fear of the threat which mass society poses to the ruling elite. If we add to this the dark shadows cast by the nuclear bomb, it will easily be understood how the fear thus engendered could be yoked to acquiescence in, or active support for, Cold War policies.

If I have anticipated a little, it is to point to the final implications of this ideology. I do not suggest that there is a direct connection between modernist literature and political attitudes of this kind. The works of Joyce and Kafka were written long before; and Robert Musil, for example, is known to have been a strong opponent of Nazism. We are not here concerned with directly political attitudes, but rather with the ideology underlying these artists' presentation of reality. The practical political conclusions drawn by the individual writer are of secondary interest. What matters is whether his view of the world, as expressed in his writings, connives at that modern nihilism from which both Fascism and Cold War ideology draw their strength.

There is a close connection between such a view of the world and the rejection of a socialist perspective. We are not concerned with academic discussions about the correctness or otherwise of socialist theory; this need have little bearing on a writer's understanding and portrayal of his age. It is a writer's actual experience of life that interests us. For Heine, on his sickbed, this problem was no less existential than for the hero of Dostoevsky's short story. And it is certainly no less so for the contemporary writer. His, and his heroes', most immediate experience is of their isolation in a world which has become increasingly abstract, uniform, technological. At first these new forces seemed to threaten only his individual culture. Later, they were seen to undermine the foundations of his moral and physical being. Finally, in the nuclear age, the perspective became the destruction of mankind itself.

Every writer has now to face the challenge of this perspective —whether or not he is aware of its social and historical circumstances. Many individual reactions seem at first sight to represent no more than the personal experience of the writers in question. And they are, of course, personal in the sense that all individual experience is unique, that a man cannot jump over his own shadow. But art implies a relation between the artist and the outer world. Indeed, whatever the private opinion of the artist,

63

a relation of some kind is inevitable. And no less inevitable is the imposition of a certain level of generalization on the subject-matter; whether he will or no, every writer describes the condition of mankind. The present social condition of mankind is at the root of even the most abstract, the most solipsistic vision of the future. And since, in the age of imperialism, of world war and world revolution, no search for a valid perspective can overlook socialism, we are entitled to guess at a rejection of socialism behind the fashionable condition of *angst*.

Put in general terms this may sound paradoxical. But examination of individual cases tends to confirm it. We have already encountered Gottfried Benn's notion of *'doppelleben'*, of statism (as against dynamics). In his essay, *Can artists change the world?*, Benn examines this problem without mystification or modernist obscurantism—indeed with a surprisingly oldfashioned lucidity.

> I am struck by the thought that it might be more revolutionary and worthier of a vigorous and active man to teach his fellow-men this simple truth: you are what you are and you will never be different; this is, was, and always will be your life. He who has money, lives long; he who has authority, can do no wrong; he who has might, establishes right. Such is history! Ecce historia! Here is the present; take of its body, eat, and die.

The triviality of this, its portentous, affectedly paradoxical tone need not be enlarged on. But it may serve as a key to some of Benn's darker utterances. It may explain the cynicism which led Benn to tolerate the social evils of his time—even collaborating with Hitler—causing him to justify the most dishonourable courses of action as morally permissible, or even desirable. If men and society are basically unchangeable, what other course is there but to collaborate with the powers that be? Seen in this light, Benn's static view of the world is the more easily understandable.

Other modernist pronouncements may be clothed in more mystical language; but they come to the same thing. The German writer Alfred Andersch, for instance, sees—not without justi-

modification / alteration of strict Marxist stance

fication—the emergence of abstract art as a 'reaction, instinctive or conscious, against the corruption of idea into ideology'. Its contemporary triumph he explains in this way: 'Since the danger of a relapse into totalitarianism is always present, abstract art retains its topicality.' What is meant by the transformation of idea into ideology? Above all, I think, a rejection of socialism. Socialism has forced a bourgeoisie which long since ceased to be revolutionary to reconsider the social roots and consequences of 'ideas'. Traditional bourgeois culture proceeded on the assumption that ideas were not relevant to social or political problems. The dominant view was that they not only could not, but should not, have such relevance. True, men of prophetic insight like Heine and Dostoevsky saw that the advent of socialism would give ideas a new importance and a new relation to reality —or, rather, that socialism would take up the threads of the tradition of the bourgeoisie itself. For nobody doubted, in the 17th and 18th centuries, that the ideas of Hobbes and Milton, of Diderot and Rousseau, strongly influenced, in conjunction with the social movements of the time, men's decisions and actions. It was only later, when the bourgeoisie had won its battle, and the proletariat was still politically and ideologically weak, that the condition which Andersch idealizes came to rule supreme.

Socially speaking, this corruption of idea into ideology has two faces. First, individual ideas are inextricably linked with the social class whose aspirations they express. Second, the struggle between conflicting ideas is ultimately decided by the outcome of the conflict between social classes. This new state of affairs, the renewed relevance of ideas in practical politics, was not properly understood by the bourgeois intelligentsia until the First World War. When, after 1917, the revolutionary outbreaks suddenly revealed that this relation had already existed for some time, the bourgeoisie were forced to face up to the phenomenon. Since bourgeois ideology, however, had at its disposal no ideas of the same calibre as socialism, it generated the 'ideologies'—in the pejorative sense of the term—of Hitlerism and, later, of nuclear

too broad

catastrophists, whose cynical logic can be found in James Burnham. Then, by way of self-defence, socialism too was declared an 'ideology'.

Inevitably, the leading bourgeois intellectuals were forced to take these changes into account in their writing. And yet, in spite of the evident urgency of the task, there has not yet appeared a system of ideas which could be successfully opposed to socialism. The most typical reactions are either cynicism, as with Gottfried Benn, or a panic-stricken *angst* in the face of Nothingness, leading to the wholesale rejection both of new social forces and of new methods to defend the old society. Andersch is right to imply that abstract art is not wholly without content, that it represents a revolt against what he calls 'ideology'. I have shown what is involved in the process which Andersch, without admittedly fully grasping it, attempts to describe. But it is all too evident that the end-product of this flight from the reality of the present day must be a form of nihilism. Once a commitment to the realities of the age is refused, human content disappears.

In his essay on Beckett, the French critic Maurice Nadeau in effect follows up Andersch's point. Beckett's literary production, he says, took a course which made him 'abandon the conventional fields of literature and penetrate deeper and deeper into that zone of darkness, into that border region where language fails, where life and death meet, where existence and consciousness dissolve and the explorer's path leads to the ante-chamber of silence, of pure reality'. Nadeau, too, speaks of a 'protest'; but this protest is 'voiced by nobody, it has no aim, no reason'. Again: 'enveloped in eternal nothingness, we are no more than bubbles that burst on the surface of a muddy pool, producing that faint sound we call existence.' He sums up: 'with Beckett, triumphant nihilism penetrates into the work of art itself, dissolving the thing it creates into a fog of meaninglessness. In the end, the author has not only made plain his intention not to say anything; he has succeeded in not saying anything. The sound of his voice in our ears is our own voice sought for and found at last.' Here is the logical conclusion of that movement to whose starting-point Andersch drew our attention.

Of course, there are many bourgeois writers who have grasped the implications of this process quite clearly and do not belittle it by indulging in a comfortable nihilism. Louis Bromfield, to take an example at random, attempted in his novel *Mr. Smith* a portrayal of Babbitt twenty years on. The book is of no great artistic merit; but it has some relevance to our investigation. Bromfield noted that in the course of two decades Babbitt's social position had changed considerably: 'His particular features and his particular problems have been undermined by disease and mental confusion without the victim's knowing it. Babbitt was crude in his way, but healthy.' (This is not, perhaps, entirely true. Sinclair Lewis had already pointed out the inherent morbidity of the type.) Now, according to Bromfield, disease is rampant, covering ever greater areas of American life. He remarks, 'In my view, our society is diseased because it is composed of stupid, gutless, extraverted individuals who frequent clubs, gambling houses, brothels, nightclubs, and bars because they are scared . . . They are obsessed with movies, with television, with sport; they are in the grip of a deep, instinctive fear. But fear of what?' His novel, which describes the downfall of Mr. Smith, sets out to find the answer.

Bromfield's novel hints unexpectedly at an inner connection between Babbitt and the ethics of modernism. His hero remembers an incident (a drinking and whoring excursion to escape the tedium of family life): 'When I think of this trip I always think of one of those surrealist paintings which show a maze of narrow streets with dazzling neon signs blazing "Pleasure Haunt" or "The Wild Man". From narrow alley-ways and entrances, innumerable phantom arms reach out and pull you from your course. It is how the world appears to a drunken man.' Bromfield explains how Mr. Smith, during a critical phase of his life, comes to prefer Proust to all other writers: Proust is the only writer in whose work 'boredom and fascination are in perfect balance'. Mr. Smith's affection for Proust is not at all literary: 'I discovered in him a life which, though decadent, was as rich and fascinating as my own everyday routine, from the day I first saw myself in the mirror, was mechanical, sterile, dreary.' This suggests, incidentally, that modernist art does not necessarily have a minority appeal. Modernist literature glorifies, with sophisticated artistry, phenomena which must otherwise appear nightmarish to the intellectual who has no perspective of the future. While traditional critical realism transforms the positive and negative elements of bourgeois life into 'typical' situations and reveals them for what they are, modernism exalts bourgeois life's very baseness and emptiness with its aesthetic devices. This tendency began with Naturalism, and has since become widespread, both as regards progressive reduction of content and increasing technical refinement.

In his novel, Bromfield touches on an important problem facing the bourgeois artist. The possibility of realism, as we know, is bound up with that minimal hope of a change for the better offered by bourgeois society. We have seen that in modernist art this perspective disappears altogether. The structure of *L'Education Sentimentale* shows that Flaubert had anticipated this development. The realistic part of the novel ends during the night on the barricades, as Frédéric Moreau watches Dussardier fall, crying 'Vive la republique!', and recognizes in the police agent his former 'radical' comrade Sénécal. The realistic novel is done with; Frédéric Moreau begins his *'Recherche du temps perdu'*.

The end of Bromfield's novel points back once more to Sinclair Lewis; this time not to *Babbitt* but to *Arrowsmith*. The subject of that novel was the position of the scientist under American capitalism. Lewis proposed that those scientists who wished to avoid corruption should escape to the solitude of the forests. Bromfield's hero, too, runs away from a society whose problems he cannot solve: he perishes miserably on a desert island during the Second World War. The difference between the endings of the two novels points to the changes that have come over society in the twenty years Bromfield surveys. Sinclair Lewis uses a mistaken, and certainly untypical, social perspective which does nevertheless give a faithful picture of preceding social developments. With Bromfield the same perspective is the symbol of an ineluctable, total fiasco.

This somewhat negative background had to be sketched in to complete our survey of perspective in bourgeois realism up to the present day. Not a few writers of the transitional period tried to give their encounter with the new situation conceptual form. Ibsen, for example, said: 'My concern is to put questions, not to supply answers.' And Chekhov declared: 'Only the question a writer puts must be reasonable. In many cases, even with Tolstoy, the answers are unreasonable. But that does not invalidate the work in question as long as it is based on a reasonable question.' The instances we have drawn from Sinclair Lewis serve to illustrate these remarks. I have already said why I think the solution in *Arrowsmith* is mistaken; and the note on which *Babbitt* ends —the sons will find the answers to the questions their fathers found too difficult—is altogether too naïve. And yet Ibsen and Chekhov are not wrong. To reject the perspective offered by Sinclair Lewis in his two novels is not to disregard what was nevertheless achieved in them.

The connection should now be apparent between Chekhov's 'reasonable question' and our earlier conclusion that a wholesale rejection of socialism will prevent the writer from giving a realistic account of the modern world. A view of the world based on chaos and *angst* presupposes the elimination of all social categories. Objective reality, we found, in the modernist writing we examined, is subjectivized and robbed of its historicity. Yet, while chaos and *angst* are the inevitable consequences of such subjectivization, their specific content, mood and ideological basis are determined by the social conditions in which the intellectual finds himself. Rejecting with passion or cynicism a socialist perspective, he fails to answer its challenge, refusing both an ideological apology for imperialism and any attempt to find a new perspective for capitalism. Even Koestler, that passionate opponent of Marxism, admitted that after his break with the Party he felt 'God's throne was empty'. The sharp discrepancy between the official ideologies of modern imperialism (Hitler's social demagogy, Burnham's managerial revolution, Democracy versus Communism etc.), and the ideology that underlies so much of contemporary bourgeois literature, is a most significant feature of our time.

That is why both our adaptation of Chekhov's 'reasonable question' and our apparently rather negative conclusion—that non-rejection of socialism is a sufficient basis for realism—are relevant and important. We must not, though, lose sight of the historical nature of our criterion; we are concerned with concrete tendencies, evolving out of actual societies, not with two rigidly opposed metaphysical entities. In my view, the criterion has increasing relevance in our study of the contemporary world; but I would admit that intellectual and social development varies in pace from country to country. There are, even in Europe, countries where feudalism is still powerful; in these the writer in opposition can still conceive of the new society in a bourgeois perspective. We have only to think of Lorca's magnificent *Bernarda Alba's House*, strikingly similar in style and theme to some of Ostrovsky's plays, and yet undeniably an organic product of modern Spanish society. In the nature of the case, such examples are comparatively rare in contemporary European literature. But they are numerous among the backward nations now attaining independence. It is perilous to generalize here; developments in India, for instance, show that socialism may figure among the forces working against medievalism. The unusual character of this social evolution will no doubt give rise to equally unusual literary developments, not to be fitted into any of our existing abstract categories.

But in treating literary developments even in highly-developed capitalist societies we must not forget that we are dealing with developments in history; and historical study demands concrete examples. I referred, earlier, to Sinclair Lewis. His perspective is unquestionably, indeed exclusively, bourgeois. Where their illusions are the main theme ('things like that can't happen to us

70

...'), the book is condemned to mediocrity. But where they are no more than a rather abstract perspective, Chekhov's notion of the 'reasonable question' appears to be justified—and justified very much in the spirit of our argument. For Sinclair Lewis' views do not amount to a rejection of socialism; at most, he drops the occasional ironic remark about such manifestations of socialism as he knew.

With Joseph Conrad, matters are rather more complex. Conrad was firmly opposed to socialism; and this opposition is evident in some of his writings, often causing a certain distortion (*The Nigger of the Narcissus, Under Western Eyes*). Yet in his best writings a strange phenomenon is observable: his faith in capitalism is such that the narrative does not even touch on its social implications. Conrad's heroes are confronted with exclusively personal, moral conflicts, in which their individual strength or weakness is revealed. Put in more general terms these conflicts might have attained a wider significance; but such generalization is excluded by the method of narration. This gives Conrad's work its finished, self-sufficient quality, but it also prevents him from portraying the totality of life; he is really a short-story writer rather than a novelist. *Typhoon* or *The Shadow Line* are famous examples; but even *Lord Jim* is, despite its length, essentially a long short-story. Thus Conrad's 'reasonable question', though excluding the most important social problems of his time, makes possible that 'triumph of realism' we find in him. It eliminated just those ideological elements which might have inhibited a truthful description of the life of his age.

Our interest centres, then, on the relation between ideology (in the sense of *Weltanschauung*) and artistic creation. Ideology has here a double significance. There are, first, a writer's conscious views about life and the problems of his time. Second, there is the understanding and portrayal of these things in his work. It was Engels who pointed out that the two might actually be diametrically opposed (I may refer the reader to my analysis of Tolstoy and Balzac in *Studies in European Realism*). This opposition takes different forms at different periods; and, even at one

71

and the same period, the opposition varies according to the personality and views of the writer in question. I want at this point, though, to reject the opposition of perception and emotion which has become so fashionable. This, though it may indeed occur in individual writers, cannot but have a bad effect on their work. Experience shows that, in any artistically fruitful opposition, both poles are invested with perception-based-on-emotion and emotion-become-perception—Heine's work is a good example of this.

It would be interesting to examine Hemingway, Steinbeck, or Thomas Wolfe in this light; bearing in mind that the analysis must always be geared to the specific character of a writer's production. Our examination of Conrad is only one example; it should not be taken as a model. But I think the relevance of our criterion could be established in all these cases. Thomas Mann's artistic development, illustrates too, the historical nature of our criterion. *Buddenbrooks* still belongs, of course, to Mann's early period. But directly before and during the First World War Mann began to introduce socialism into the world portrayed in his writings. And, from the *Magic Mountain* onwards, socialism never ceases to be a central intellectual and compositional element.

The negatively formulated 'reasonable question' of contemporary realism—no *a priori* rejection of socialism—has as its complement another negative imperative: the will to overcome *angst* and chaos. I have tried to show that these form the essential content of modernism. This vision of the world as chaos results from the lack of a humanist social perspective. The self-deception from which modernism suffers in this respect is based on a peculiar, and contradictory, piece of dogmatism. To modernists, though they are almost without exception supporters of extreme subjectivism, the static nature of reality, and the senselessness of its surface phenomena, are absolute truths requiring no proof. Naturally, phenomena in the outer world, governed by their own immanent laws, exist outside human consciousness. But the human subject plays a part in the understanding of particular phenomena and in the perception of their interrelatedness. As Hegel said, 'He who looks at the world rationally, finds in it a rational pattern; the two processes are one.'

In the same way, the reason for the part played in modernist art by *angst* is not to be found in the dogma that reality is chaos. Rather, inability to grasp the new pattern of social development leads to an *angst*-ridden view of reality. *Angst*, of course, derives from an experience in the outer world; but this experience is of its nature subjective and results from a certain way of looking at reality. Kierkegaard, the prophet of this experience, comments: '... Nothingness, the object of *angst*, gradually becomes an entity.... The Nothingness that results from *angst* is a complex of subjective fears, reflecting one another and gradually closing in on the individual....' We see that, contrary to the dogma, *angst* precedes chaos in modernist ideology. Chaos is the consequence of *angst*; and *angst* in turn is the product of social experience—the effect, specifically, of the social structure of imperialism on the bourgeois intelligentsia. Rejection of socialism as a possible perspective involves closing one's eyes to the future; the individual then accepts *angst* and chaos as a permanent condition. It is not, I think, necessary to analyse the ideology further. Earlier in this study I contrasted those two fundamentally opposed ontologies, Aristotelianism and Existentialism. Let us now look at the matter in a rather broader context.

Angst, as a dominant existential condition, leads to an impoverishment, reduction and distortion of the image of man and of described reality. It excludes everything lying beyond its own radius, and particularly—a natural consequence of its origin—everything that invests man and his environment with social significance. This process continues through the imperialist period. It is latent in Naturalism, reaching a culmination in the later works of Strindberg. Earlier, in the plays of the young Maeterlinck, it had already found authentic form. *Angst*, in the shape of a disturbing premonition or vague *sehnsucht*, had been the effective content of much Naturalistic literature; with Maeterlinck it became the exclusive content, displacing all other aspirations. Beckett's *Waiting for Godot*, whatever variations it may offer in style and mood, is essentially very close to early Maeterlinck.

A new feature in the later stages of this process is the increasing exclusiveness, the radical, almost brutal elimination of social significance. Take, for instance, D. H. Lawrence's reduction of erotic relations to phallic sexuality, or the even more extreme version of this reduction in Henry Miller. The German critic Helmut Uhlig gives this description of Miller's world: 'Contempt for work, drink as a drug, sexual intercourse as the raison d'etre of existence, promiscuity as a way of life, reliance on all manner of violent stimuli.' And he goes on to quote Miller on his own experience of life: 'The world came to resemble a pornographic film, with impotence as its tragic theme.' Uhlig points out that similarities can be found in the works, say, of Broch, Kafka, and Musil. Impotence is thought of not so much as a physical failure, but rather as 'a man's emotional failure to establish contact with a woman; a betrayal of woman, who—with Miller—is degraded into a mere object, and valued for her sexual capacity alone'. These comments, coming as they do from a non-socialist, confirm our point. The tendency I am describing is, of course, a good deal more complex in writers of greater talent and intelligence than Henry Miller. And the reduction of which I have spoken does not necessarily relate, as Beckett's example shows, only to sexuality.

Yet this reduction is here the ultimate determinant of literary style. Earlier in this study I discussed the question of narrative detail and its place in the totality of the work of art and concluded that the rejection of a selective principle must lead the modernist writer to naturalism, even where the experimental form would lead one to expect the opposite. We can now take these findings a stage further: the selective principle which apparently underlies modernist writing is no more than a crude selection of content, on the one hand, and of technique, on the other. It is not a selection applied to the totality of the reality to be described. In genuine selection, insignificant data are

74

eliminated and significant data stressed. In modernism, purely formal principles of selection lead to a fragmentation of human nature (Henry Miller, for instance, ignores everything in human nature that cannot be related to sexuality). A pseudo-selection of this kind degrades the human image, eliminating much that is of the essence of man.

The problem of narrative detail, of naturalism, has thus to be seen in a wider context. Since human nature is not finally separable from social reality, each narrative detail will be significant to the extent that it expresses the dialectic between man-as-individual and man-as-social-being. It is these tensions and contradictions both within the individual, and underlying the individual's relation with his fellow human beings—all of which tensions increase in intensity with the evolution of capitalism— that must form the subject-matter of contemporary realism. The realistic writer must seek the nodal points of these conflicts, determine where they are at their most intense and most typical, and give suitable expression to them. Good realistic detail often in itself implies a judgment on these conflicts. The question of what we mean by the *norm*, and by *distortion*, is also involved.

These categories—norm and distortion—can be used to determine an individual's relation to society; but they can only do this if the literary technique allows of equal treatment being given to both aspects of human nature. A realistic work of art, however rich in descriptive detail, is always opposed to naturalism. But an artistic method which reduces the dialectical—social-and-individual—totality of human existence must relapse, as we have seen, into naturalistic arbitrariness. It will then be incapable of depicting distortion in human nature or in the individual's relation to his environment—incapable, that is, of seeing distortion as distortion.

Once again we observe the profoundly anti-artistic character of modernism. The historical legitimation of modernism derives from the fact that the distortion of human nature, the anti-artistic character of human relationships, is an inevitable product of capitalist society. Yet since modernism portrays this

75

distortion without critical detachment, indeed devises stylistic techniques which emphasize the necessity of distortion in any kind of society, it may be said to distort distortion further. By attributing distortion to reality itself, modernism dismisses the counter-forces at work in reality as ontologically irrelevant. It is easy to understand that the experience of the contemporary capitalist world does produce, especially among intellectuals, *angst*, nausea, a sense of isolation, and despair. Indeed, a view of the world which *excluded* these emotions would prevent the present-day artist from depicting his world truthfully. The question is not: is *x* present in reality? But rather: does *x* represent the whole of reality? Again, the question is not; should *x* be excluded from literature? But rather: should we be content to leave it at *x*?

We are brought back once again to questions of ideology. If a writer takes *angst* to be the basic experience of modern man, his attitude towards the life of his time betrays an uncritical naïvety. 'Naïvety' I want here to be understood in a philosophical sense. I went into this concept in my published correspondence with Anna Seghers about realism over two decades ago. I meant by it an attitude which excluded critical detachment, which registered the phenomena of life naïvely, which stuck to first impressions. This attitude, I showed then, may be combined with rigorous scientific investigation—though it will be a scientific activity uncritical of its own assumptions. We cannot go further into the question here—examining to what extent, for instance, this 'naïvety' is a spontaneous reaction of the artist living under capitalism, and to what extent it is deliberately furthered to prevent the artist from criticizing capitalism's presuppositions. I want merely to point out the distinction between a critical and a naïve approach in the present context, in order to clarify its philosophical basis. I would like also to recall our earlier discussion of the connection between realism—i.e. a writer's critical understanding of the world he lives in—and the struggle for peace, which is similarly based on an ideological rejection of assumptions about the inevitability of war which are based on uncritical analysis of reality. The distinction between this approach and that of modernism, which by its nature must be uncritical and naïve in its attitude to reality, should be sufficiently evident.

Franz Kafka is the classic example of the modern writer at the mercy of a blind and panic-stricken *angst*. His unique position he owes to the fact that he found a direct, uncomplex way of communicating this basic experience; he did so without having recourse to formalistic experimentation. Content is here the immediate determinant of aesthetic form—that is why Kafka belongs with the great realistic writers. Indeed, he is one of the greatest of all, if we consider how few writers have ever equalled his skill in the imaginative evocation of the concrete novelty of the world. Never was the quality of Kafka's achievement more striking or more needed than at the present day, when so many writers fall for slick experimentation. The impact of Kafka's work derives not only from his passionate sincerity—rare enough in our age—but also from the corresponding simplicity of the world he constructs. That is Kafka's most original achievement. Kierkegaard said, 'The greater a man's originality, the more he is at the mercy of *angst*.' Kafka, original in the Kierkegaardian sense, describes this *angst* and the fragmented world which—it is incorrectly assumed—is both its complement and its cause. His originality lies not in discovering any new means of expression but in the utterly convincing, and yet continually startling, presentation of his invented world, and of his characters' reaction to it. 'What shocks is not the monstrosity of it,' writes Theodor W. Adorno, 'but its matter-of-factness.'

The diabolical character of the world of modern capitalism, and man's impotence in the face of it, is the real subject-matter of Kafka's writings. His simplicity and sincerity are, of course, the product of complex and contradictory forces. Let us consider only one aspect. Kafka wrote at a time when capitalist society, the object of his *angst*, was still far from the high mark of its historical development. What he described and 'demonized' was not the truly demonic world of Fascism, but the world of the

Hapsburg Monarchy. *Angst*, haunting and indefinable, is perfectly reflected in this vague, ahistorical, timeless world, steeped in the atmosphere of Prague. Kafka profited from his historical position in two ways. On the one hand, his narrative detail gains from being rooted in the Austrian society of that period. On the other hand, the essential unreality of human existence, which it is his aim to convey, can be related to a corresponding sense of unreality and foreboding in the society he knew. The identification with the *condition humaine* is far more convincing than in later visions of a diabolical, *angst*-inspiring world, where so much has to be eliminated or obscured by formal experimentation to achieve the desired ahistorical, timeless image of the human condition. But this, though the reason for the astonishing impact and lasting power of Kafka's work, cannot disguise its basically allegorical character. The wonderfully suggestive descriptive detail points to a transcendent reality, to the anticipated reality—stylized into timelessness—of fully developed imperialism. Kafka's details are not, as in realism, the nodal points of individual or social life; they are cryptic symbols of an unfathomable transcendence. The stronger their evocative power, the deeper is the abyss, the more evident the allegorical gap between meaning and existence.

The counterpart to this fascinating, though ill-starred, development in modern bourgeois literature is the work of Thomas Mann. I have examined Thomas Mann's work extensively elsewhere, and shall be brief. It is only important for our purposes to work out the contrast with Kafka. Let us begin with the artistic presentation. The world of Thomas Mann is free from transcendental reference: place, time and detail are rooted firmly in a particular social and historical situation. Mann envisages the perspective of socialism without abandoning the position of a bourgeois, and without attempting to portray the newly emergent socialist societies or even the forces working towards their establishment (in the context of realism, Thomas Mann's mature attitude of acceptance and resignation, and Roger Martin du Gard's heroic failure, form an interesting opposition).

This apparently limited perspective is nevertheless of central importance in Thomas Mann's work: it is the main reason for the harmony of its proportions. Each section of a portrayed totality is placed in a concrete social context; the significance of each detail, its meaning for the evolution of society, is clearly defined. It is our world that Thomas Mann describes, the world in whose shaping we play a part, and which in turn shapes us. The deeper Thomas Mann probes into the complexity of present-day reality, the more clearly we come to understand our position in the complex evolution of mankind. Thus Thomas Mann, despite his loving attention to detail, never lapses into naturalism. For all his fascination with the dark regions of modern existence, Thomas Mann always shows up distortion for what it is, tracing its roots and its concrete origins in society.

In his study of Dostoevsky, André Gide wrote, 'Beautiful feelings make bad art', and, 'without the devil's help there would be no art'. Some of Thomas Mann's writings are based on not dissimilar views; there are parallels in his early story *Tonio Kröger*. Yet, in the same story, Mann also gives us the opposing view. The problem treated is familiar in the modern world. Thomas Mann is concerned to investigate the demonic, the underworld of the human mind, within the context of present-day society. Early in his career he realized that the artist himself is one of the main mediators of this experience. It is therefore natural that he should have followed up this early insight with increasingly rigorous studies of the problem in its social context. The examination begun with *Tonio Kröger*, ended with *Dr Faustus*. With Adrian Leverkühn, Mann's Faustus, the enquiry is concentrated on the present time, though it is a present seen in the perspective of history. The devil has to confess that, with Goethe, his assistance was strictly unnecessary, but that the social conditions of Leverkühn's time compelled the composer to seek guidance from the underworld. Yet Leverkühn's final monologue reveals the perspective of a new society, of socialism, under which the artist will be freed from his former enslavement. Indeed, the mere struggle for the social reformation

of mankind may of itself suffice to break the power of the underworld.

Gide's attitude to the problem, as we saw from the above remarks, was 'naïve', uncritical. He surrendered to the supremacy
of the underworld, greeted it even with a certain intellectual
relish, and with the customary contempt for the trivial philistinism of bourgeois existence. Gide's notion of the *action gratuite*
reflects the same view, as does his doctrine of 'sincerity'. What
in Mann is simply one legitimate theme among others—legitimate even where it is the main theme of a novel or story—becomes with Gide a doctrine governing all life and all art—and
thus distorting both. This is the crossroads where critical realism
not only parts ways with modernism, but is even forced into
opposition to it.

Between these methods, between Franz Kafka and Thomas
Mann, the contemporary bourgeois writer will have to choose.
There is no necessity for a writer to break with his bourgeois
pattern of life in making this choice between social sanity and
morbidity, in choosing the great and progressive literary traditions of realism in preference to formalistic experimentation. (Of
course, there are many writers who will choose socialism as a
way of solving their personal dilemma. I only want to emphasize
that this is not the only possible choice for the contemporary
writer.) What counts is the personal decision. Chekhov's 'reasonable question' implies, above all, a choice of direction. And
today that is determined by the question: acceptance or rejection of *angst*? Ought *angst* to be taken as an absolute, or ought it
to be overcome? Should it be considered one reaction among
others, or should it become the determinant of the *condition
humaine*? These are not primarily, of course, literary questions;
they relate to a man's behaviour and experience of life. The
crucial question is whether a man escapes from the life of his
time into a realm of abstraction—it is then that *angst* is engendered in human consciousness—or confronts modern life determined to fight its evils and support what is good in it. The
first decision leads then to another: is man the helpless victim

of transcendental and inexplicable forces, or is he a member of a human community in which he can play a part, however small, towards its modification or reform?

These problems could well be expanded and generalized; but it is not necessary to do so here. The implications of our basic question—acceptance of *angst* or rejection—are clear enough. We see here, ideologically and artistically, the root of our modern dilemma. However passionately, however sophistically, the historical origins of *angst* may be obscured, no work of art based on it can avoid—objectively speaking—guilt by association with Hitlerism and the preparations for atomic war. It is, indeed, of the nature of literature's social significance that it reflects the movements of its age even when it is—subjectively—aiming to express something very different (this opposition between subjective intention and objective compulsion is at the root of the modernist dilemma: modernism is in revolt against the anti-aestheticism of capitalism, and yet in the process revolts against art itself). *What is art? (Art only that which provides a social perspective?)*

Earlier, I quoted Adorno's remark that modern music had lost the original authenticity of *angst*. This, and similar instances, being interpreted, could well be taken as an admission of defeat in the field of nuclear war preparations, an admission of loss of ground in the Cold War, as new perspectives for peace begin to open up. Modernism, based on nihilism, is losing that suggestive power which contrived to invest Nothingness with a false objectivity. The experience of Nothingness, though distorting reality when made use of in literature, did possess a certain subjective authenticity. This authenticity, however, has diminished with time. Thus, as the crisis of modernism deepens, critical realism grows in importance.

Let me repeat: these changes are primarily changes in human behaviour, in ideological attitude; only by this route can they affect literature. Moreover, I would like the reader to recall what I said earlier about the peculiar ideological pattern underlying the Peace Movement: how it allows great ideological divergencies, even contradictions, holding together differing

81

approaches by a certain community of opinion on human, social, and international problems. Chekhov's 'reasonable question', which we found to be the basis of all realistic literature, is the theoretical link between a community of opinion of this kind and the creative process itself.

It is evident that changes of this sort must be complex and contradictory. They may involve the gradual transformation of a writer's understanding of the social and historical reality of his time (Thomas Mann, for instance, during and after the First World War). A writer's earlier views will not necessarily be abandoned in their entirety, even if these views are really inseparable from the abandoned intellectual position (e.g. Thomas Mann's continued attachment to Schopenhauer and Nietzsche). One result, in the field of theory, is likely to be the partial break-up of the earlier ideology—as with Sartre, whose political views are often inconsistent with his unrevised existentialist premises. A writer faced with this dilemma may yet succeed in formulating his 'reasonable question' on the basis of his new position. The problems he leaves unsolved may appear in his work as truthful reflections of contradictions actually present in society. Sartre's work provides evidence of this.

Apparent inconsistencies in a writer's view of the world, reflected in his work, should never be treated dogmatically. The main thing—and it is no small thing—is whether the writer's view is able to include—or, better, demands—a dynamic, complex, analytical rendering of social relationships, or whether it leads to loss of perspective and historicity. We are confronted once again with an alternative—acceptance of *angst* or rejection—and with all the consequences flowing from that alternative. This dilemma is the key to the assessment of modern literature.

It is applicable, not least, in matters of style. Earlier, in talking of the historical and aesthetic significance of certain stylistic phenomena, I rejected any rigid distinction, on formal principles alone, between bourgeois realism and decadent anti-realism. In a period of transition, when the rejection of old beliefs and the formulation of new beliefs is a continuous process, this negative principle of judgment becomes more, rather than less, important. Crucial, for the critic, is the determination of the direction in which a writer is moving, not the detection of stylistic idiosyncrasies. This is not to say that style is unimportant. On the contrary, I maintain that the more closely we combine an examination of the ideology informing a writer's work with an examination of the specific form given to a specific content, the better our analysis will be. That is to say, the critic must establish by examination of the work whether a writer's view of the world is based on the acceptance or rejection of *angst*, whether it involves a flight from reality or a willingness to face up to it.

The more *angst* predominates, the greater will be the levelling effect. We have seen this in the case of abstract and concrete potentiality. But the loss of any concern for ethical complexity, for the problems of society, is part of the same process. The question of the 'authenticity' of human behaviour is no longer important. Particularly in modernist writing, the differing reactions of human beings come to seem insignificant in the face of 'metaphysical' *angst* (and of the increasing pressures of conformity). The fact that in the midst of this 'permanent revolution', this endless 'revaluation of all values', there were writers of major talent who clung to the standards of nineteenth-century realism is, therefore, of ethical as much as of artistic significance. These writers' attitudes sprang from the ethical conviction that though changes in society modify human nature, they do not abolish it. Once again, Roger Martin du Gard is the classic example. The conviction is evident, not only in his thinking about literature, but also in the values inherent in his work. We have only to contrast the tragic authenticity of his Jacques Thibault with the inauthenticity of his Fontanin, who embodies the Gidean ethic.

But Martin du Gard is by no means the only example. The best work of Eugene O'Neill, an experimentalist from his expressionist period onward, was done under the influence of nineteenth-century, Ibsenite drama. I am not implying that O'Neill, either philosophically or artistically, was an imitator of Ibsen. On the contrary, he does away with Ibsen's moralizing and his weakness for romantic symbolism. The tragicomedy of Ibsen's stern imperatives, too, is foreign to O'Neill's drama. O'Neill's tragicomedy has been through the school of Chekhov. The ethical-dramatic dialectic is no longer that between absolute imperatives and the impossibility of their realization. We are now concerned with the scope and possibilities of human action as such; O'Neill's subject is man himself, his subjectively tragic and yet objectively comic situation. Again, to say that O'Neill drew inspiration from Chekhov is not to accuse him of imitation. The America he portrays is, sociologically, that described by his contemporaries—though he often, to win dramatic distance, sets the scene in the America of the past. But he is interested not so much in the way human beings can be manipulated in the name of 'Freedom', as in whether, and how, the human substance can survive such a process. O'Neill wishes to know whether a man is in the last analysis responsible for his own actions or is the plaything of psychological and social forces over which he has no control. His American Electra acknowledges responsibility for her actions with tragic pride; the integrity of human personality is preserved, though at great cost. But such a situation is unusual in O'Neill. More often, the authentic and the inauthentic are inextricably interwoven in his characters— the accent falling more and more frequently on the latter. That is O'Neill's originality. Seeing the situation as he does, he is yet able to affirm, with his own brand of tragicomic defiance, a basic integrity in human personality. For all the apparent gloom, this is the message of later dramas like *A Moon for the Misbegotten* or *A Touch of the Poet*. In other words, O'Neill's return to Ibsen and Chekhov is at the same time a protest against the dominance of modernism and a confession of faith in the future of humanity.

Stylistically, Elsa Moranti, the Italian novelist, might seem a far cry from O'Neill. Her technique is very much of the present day; little would seem to associate her with the literature of the nineteenth century. All the more striking, then, the philosophical and ethical affinities apparent in her treatment of motive and perspective. Life and its turmoils, in her work, are the threshing-floor where the authentic is winnowed from the inauthentic. Her best-known novel is entitled, significantly, *Lies and Magic*. The plot is intelligent, finely symbolic, excellently suited to the problems she examines. She describes in the opening chapters the inner revolt of a human being, caught in a net of magic and unreality, against these entangling forces. The *'recherche du temps perdu'* is here no more than a prelude, an introductory evocation of the past—but of the past as it really was, and as none of the characters in the story could have known it from personal experience. Thus, the true subject-matter of the story, the world of *temps retrouvé* is not reduced to a mere *état d'âme*. The motives are derived from actual life; they are the passions, though informed by 'false consciousness', that are at the root of men's actions. The reader—as in the traditional epic —is granted an omniscience allowing him to see the totality of the world portrayed. The winnowing of the authentic from the inauthentic is not effected by the personal intervention of the author. It is the concrete contradictions embodied in her characters, their complex interrelations, that accomplish the process. The novel becomes, in fact, a grandiose parable of modern man's ethical condition. This parabolic quality might seem to yield a point of contact with modernism. But the resemblance does not go very deep; it is confined to the depiction of general background rather than to the portrayal of individuals. The social pressures on the individual are never abstractly conceived—the chief temptation of the parabolic form. The characters' rootedness in their milieu is rendered with remarkable skill. Purely individual and purely class characteristics, carefully distinguished, are yet fused in a unity rarely found outside classical realism. The parabolic quality of the whole is *'aufgehoben'*, in the Hegelian sense, in three ways: it is 'cancelled out', yet also preserved; and at the same time it is raised to a higher level—a level where life,

85

and philosophical reflection upon it, form a dialectical unity.

Thomas Wolfe's novel *You Can't Go Home Again* deserves a brief mention here, since it illustrates the turning point in his life so well. Wolfe has described how he began his career as a disciple of Joyce; but his substitution of the *monologue intérieur* for the formal rigours of plot has, in actual fact, a quite different character. It is never a mere stream of consciousness behind which objective reality disappears. The real subject-matter, even of the young Thomas Wolfe, is the reality of modern America; and the stream of consciousness is no more than a part of this objectively-rendered whole. Wolfe's early style, still Joycean but already pointing beyond Joyce, must be seen in relation to his general philosophical stance. Wolfe was passionately involved in the life of his time; but his hates and enthusiasms were on a level of pure emotion. Joyce's technique enabled him to react to and record, emotionally and subjectively, the life around him. But he went beyond Joyce in that he was not the uninvolved spectator of his age. Rather, he was impelled by—admittedly largely unconscious—ethical and social motives either furiously to reject or furiously to affirm what he saw. In his last novel, this unawareness of his own motives has gone. The experience of the Depression, and later of Nazi Germany, revealed to him the make-up of the society of which he was a member. This new understanding enabled him to order and clarify his emotions. The result is the magnificent portrait—particularly in the first half of the book—of America on the eve of the 1929 disaster. But the second half of the book shows that the awareness was not yet complete. By giving his fictive hero certain features obviously taken from Sinclair Lewis, Wolfe attempts to set up a new ideal of what the writer should be. His hero achieves what the young Wolfe had longed for—fame. But fame, when found, is not enough to slake his ambition. Wolfe offers, then, a somewhat abstract solution—he argues that 'one can and should better the human lot', that there is a greater wisdom than the wisdom of Ecclesiastes. This enables him to give, for instance, splendidly realized descriptions of conditions in the

Third Reich. But the second half of the novel is artistically chaotic and leans far too heavily, towards the end, on mere discussion. It must be said, nevertheless, that Thomas Wolfe's death robbed us of a realistic writer of the first promise.

In Brecht's development, too, traditional realism played an important role. I have no space here to examine Brecht's work at length. We must begin with Brecht's middle period, the period of his turning towards communism, of *The Measures Taken* and of his adaptation of Gorky's *Mother*. Brecht's political didacticism, his attempt to impose intellectual schemata on the spectator, turned his characters into mere spokesmen. He based his new aesthetic on a contempt for cheap theatrical emotionalism. The full blast of his hatred was directed towards the 'culinary' aspects of the contemporary bourgeois theatre. And he seized on the theory of *Einfühlung* as the source of much of the bad art of the time. Now there is no doubt that Brecht, despite his exaggerations, was right to reject this particular theory. But he made the then not uncommon mistake—implicit in Wilhelm Worringer's original formulation of the theory—of assuming that *Einfühlung* was fundamental to traditional aesthetics. The boss's secretary may 'identify', through *Einfühlung*, with her opposite number on the screen; and the young man about town may identify with, say, Schnitzler's *Anatol*. But no one surely has ever, in this sense, 'identified' with Antigone or King Lear. The truth is, Brecht's dramatic theories were the product of an—at the time, quite justified—local polemic. Brecht's actual dramatic practice changed radically after the rise to power of Hitler, during his long years of exile. But he never subjected his theories to revision. I have no space to investigate the problem in detail. But two poems, written during that exile, may serve to indicate the changes I have in mind :

A wooden Japanese mask hangs on my wall
The mask of an angry demon, covered with gold.
With fellow-feeling I see
The swollen veins in the forehead, showing
What a strenuous business it is to be angry.

87

Or these lines from the marvellous poem *To Posterity*:

> Yet we know too well,
> Hatred of evil
> Can distort the features,
> Rage at injustice
> Make the voice hoarse. Alas, we
> Who wished to make room for friendliness
> Could not ourselves be friendly.

We see here how ethical preoccupations, a concern for the inner life and motivation of his characters, began to loom larger in Brecht's mind. Not that his central political and social preoccupations were displaced. On the contrary, the effect of this change was to give them greater depth, range and intensity. And even the greatest admirers of Brecht's dramaturgy must admit that many plays of this period—*The Rifles of Señora Carrar* or *The Life of Galileo*—evidence a partial return to despised Aristotelean aesthetics. Be that as it may, let us briefly turn our attention to those plays—*Mother Courage, The Caucasian Chalk Circle, The Good Woman of Setzuan*—which do not thus return to traditional norms. These plays are indeed *Lehrstücke*, products of epic theatre; the anti-Aristotelean intention, the calculated use of alienation-effects, is undeniable. But if we compare these plays with, say, *The Measures Taken* we see that the over-simplified schema of that play has given way to a complex dialectic of good and evil. Problems of society have become problems of humanity, subsuming the inner conflicts and contradictions of the warring parties. Where Brecht's characters had once been spokesmen for political points of view, they are now multi-dimensional. They are living human beings, wrestling with conscience and with the world around them. Allegory has acquired flesh and blood; it has been transformed into a true dramatic typology. Alienation-effect ceases to be the instrument of an artificial, abstract didacticism; it makes possible literary achievement of the highest order. All great drama, after all, must find means to transcend the limited awareness of the characters presented on the stage. It must express the general philosophical theme, represented in concrete terms by the action, in adequate poetic form (this is the function of the chorus in Aeschylus and Sophocles, and of the monologue in *Hamlet*, *Othello*, and *Lear*). It is this aspect that predominates in the later Brecht, a direct consequence of his new concern for ethical complexity, of his search for a multi-dimensional typology. That Brecht clung to his earlier theories should not conceal from us this fundamental change. Even the scenic structure of Brecht's plays begins to approximate to the Shakespearean model. The break with the '*milieu*-theatre', with the 'atmospheric' ambience of the older stage, is really a break with naturalism. It is a return to a dramaturgy aiming both at a typology that displays the full range of human complexity and at the creation of living human beings grappling with the forces of their environment. The mature Brecht, by overcoming his earlier, one-sided theories, had evolved into the greatest realistic playwright of his age. And the most influential, too, for good and for bad. Indeed, Brecht's influence shows once again how misleading it is to argue from the theory to the work and not from the work, its structure and intellectual content, to the theory. For Brecht's theories lead both to the pretentious, empty experimentalism of Ionesco and to topical, realistic drama like Dürrenmatt's *The Visit*. The confusion to which this gave rise—the result of a formalistic over-emphasis on one element abstracted from literature—is still remarkably widespread and influential (that Brecht was a socialist writer, both in personal ideology and literary practice, in no way contradicts what I have said here. His influence has been, and is, chiefly effective in the struggle between critical realism and modernist anti-realism).

The critic today must put aside his personal preferences and use all his tact, energy and discretion in evaluating those works of literature which fight against old-established prejudices and strive to open up new areas of experience. To take one example: it is true to say that naturalism represents—compared with true realism—a decline and an impoverishment. In existing conditions, however, a naturalistic novel like Norman Mailer's *The*

Naked and the Dead marks a step forward from the trackless desert of abstractions towards a portrayal of the actual suffering of actual people during the Second World War. Arbitrary though much of the detail is, and retrograde though the author's subsequent artistic development has been, the merits of that achievement, tentative as it was, should not be overlooked. The same may be true even where at first glance there is little evidence of realism. A case in point is *Kimmerische Fahrt*, a novel by the German writer, Werner Warsinsky. Stylistically, this is a competent exercise in the Kafka manner, using techniques evolved by Joyce and Beckett. Formally, the subject would appear to be the *condition humaine* of modernist ideology: there are the same forces working towards man's degradation and ultimate destruction. But the real focus of the book is the hero's experience of the collapse of Nazism; his fate is representative of the fate of a whole generation. The mist and darkness occluding the *angst*-ridden mind of the hero, who is running away from himself and from all contact with the outside world, are the true subject-matter of the book, not a mere stylistic device (though the opposite would seem to be true, if the book is approached from a formal angle). Again, through this mist we catch sight, from time to time, of living human beings realistically portrayed. As an account of an historical catastrophe the book is excellent. Not dissimilar is the use of dream sequences in Wolfgang Koeppen's *Treibhaus*. Here, the dreamlike atmosphere helps to establish a definite historical atmosphere, while implying a judgment on the dreamlike world of Bonn politics. In his *Tod in Rom* Koeppen goes further in the realism of his treatment of human situation and character. Many other examples, of course, could be found; but the scope of this study does not permit us to take further examples. I want only to point out that these works are the products of a period of transition, and should be investigated as such.

It is a difficult and complex task, yet it is perfectly possible, for a writer to change his attitude to himself, to his fellow human beings, and the world at large. The forces employed against him, admittedly, are enormously powerful. Nihilism and cynicism, despair and *angst*, suspicion and self-disgust are the spontaneous product of the capitalist society in which intellectuals have to live. Many factors, in education and elsewhere, are arrayed against him. Take, for instance, the view that pessimism is aristo-cratic, a worthier philosophy for an intellectual élite than faith in human progress. Or the belief that the individual—precisely as a member of an élite—must be a helpless victim of historical forces. Or the idea that the rise of mass society is an unmitigated evil. The majority of the press, highbrow and lowbrow, tends to minister to prejudices of this kind (it is their role in the cam-paign for the continuation of the Cold War). It is as if it were unworthy of the intellectual to hold other than dogmatic modernist views on life, art, and philosophy. To support realism in art, to examine the possibilities of peaceful coexistence among nations, to strive for an impartial evaluation of communism (which does not involve allegiance to it), all this may make a writer an outcast in the eyes of his colleagues and in the eyes of those on whom he depends for a livelihood. Since a writer of Sartre's standing has had to endure attacks of this kind, how much more dangerous is the situation likely to be for younger, less prominent writers.

These, and much more, are hard facts. But we must not forget that strong counter-forces are at work, particularly today; and that they are growing in strength. The writer who considers his own basic interests, those of his nation and of mankind as a whole, and who decides to work against the forces prevailing in the capitalist world, is now no longer alone. The further his explorations take him, the firmer his choice will be, and the less isolated will he feel, for he will be identifying himself with those forces in the world of his time which will one day prevail. *Marxist optimism*

The period during which Fascism rose to power, like the period of Fascist ascendancy and the subsequent Cold War period, were hardly favourable to the growth of critical realism. Neverthe-less, excellent work was done; neither physical terror nor intel-lectual pressure succeeded in preventing it. There were always critical realist writers who opposed war—in both its cold and hot manifestations—and the destruction of art and culture. Not a few works of high artistic merit emerged from the struggle. Today, the imminent defeat of Cold War policies, the new perspective of peaceful coexistence among the nations, should allow wider scope for a critical and realistic bourgeois literature. The real dilemma of our age is not the opposition between capitalism and socialism, but the opposition between peace and war. The first duty of the bourgeois intellectual has become the rejection of an all-pervading fatalistic *angst*, implying a rescue operation for humanity rather than any breakthrough to Socialism. Because it is these perspectives that confront him, the bourgeois writer today is in a better position to solve his own dilemma than he was in the past. It is the dilemma of the choice between an aesthetically appealing, but decadent modernism, and a fruitful critical realism. It is the choice between Franz Kafka and Thomas Mann.

Critical Realism and Socialist Realism

OUR ANALYSIS of critical realism would be incomplete if it were limited to the contrast between critical realism and bourgeois modernism, and not extended to the relation between critical and socialist realism. It is impossible, of course, to go into all the problems of socialist realism in this study. I shall confine myself, therefore, to the relation between the two types of realism and touch only on those aspects of socialist realism which bear on the prospects for critical realism in our time.

Let us first consider the question of *perspective* in critical and socialist realism, as we did when dealing with bourgeois realism and modernism. The perspective of socialist realism is, of course, the struggle for socialism. This perspective will vary in form and content according to the level of social development and the subject-matter. The decisive point—particularly in contrast to critical realism—is not simply the acceptance of socialism. This is possible within the framework of critical realism. An outright affirmation of socialism is not, of course, characteristic of the main body of critical realist writing (I have shown that a negative attitude, readiness to respect the perspective of socialism and not condemn it out of hand, is sufficient). And it is true that such an affirmation will remain somewhat abstract, for even where a critical realist attempts to describe socialism, his is bound to be a description *from the outside.*

That, then, is the crucial distinction. Socialist realism differs from critical realism, not only in being based on a concrete socialist perspective, but also in using this perspective to describe the forces working towards socialism *from the inside.* Socialist society is seen as an independent entity, not simply as a foil to capitalist society, or as a refuge from its dilemmas—as with those critical realists who have come closest to embracing socialism. Even more important is the treatment of those social forces leading towards socialism; scientific, as against utopian, socialism aims to locate those forces scientifically, just as socialist realism is concerned to locate those human qualities which make for the creation of a new social order. The revolt against the old order, against capitalism—the point of contact between critical realism and a socialist perspective—becomes a subordinate element in this wider context. Since perspective, as we have seen, plays a decisive role as a selective principle in literature, these considerations are of no small importance in forming the style of socialist realism.

Let us consider our first point in greater detail—description of socialism from the inside rather than from the outside. No distinction between a superficial and a profound grasp of human character is necessarily implied. Great satirists, such as Swift or Saltykov-Shchedrin, always saw character from the outside. Indeed, this refusal to enter into all the subjective complexities of the world they satirize is the presupposition of a good satirical typology. The opposition I have in mind is different. By the 'outside' method a writer obtains a typology based on the individual and his personal conflicts; and from this base he works towards wider social significance. The 'inside' method seeks to discover an Archimedian point in the midst of social contradictions, and then bases its typology on an analysis of these contradictions.

Many realistic writers use both methods; and both methods may coexist in the same work of art. Dickens is a case in point: his plebeian characters are explored from the inside, his upper- and middle-class characters from the outside. Dickens is perhaps an extreme case, but a most instructive one if we wish to study the social origins of the phenomenon. It is evident that writers will tend to present an inside picture of the class on which their own experience of society is based. All other social classes will tend to be seen from the outside. But, again, this is no more than a generalization: Tolstoy's view of the world approximates to that of the exploited Russian peasantry; yet he undoubtedly portrays the gentry, and a section of the aristocracy, from the inside.

On the other hand, only vulgar sociology conceives of class structure as something static. It is a dynamic thing, containing within itself past, present, and future of the society in question. There is a tendency for all writers to present the world of their immediate experience from the inside, and the past or future of that world (if the latter promises to be different from the present) from the outside. The great realists of course, vary in the range of their 'inside' knowledge. Shakespeare, no doubt, achieved the broadest range, depicting even the inside world of characters entirely unsympathetic to him. But many writers have deluded themselves as to their true position. Balzac's Quixotic *ancien régime* aristocracy is, unquestionably, a portrait from the inside. Yet it is a portrait done with devasting irony and critical detachment, not at all on a level with those of Alfred de Vigny or Achim von Arnim. Again, Balzac is wholly out of sympathy with his Mucingens or Gobseks; but they are drawn, nevertheless, from the inside.

With these reservations, it is clear that an 'outside' description of events in the past may attain a high degree of authenticity. In literature, as elsewhere, a critical understanding of the present is the key to the understanding of the past. In regard to the future, this is not necessarily so. In the preceding chapter I examined the modifications perspective underwent during the history of critical realism. We concluded that, for a correct assessment of the future, the perspective of socialism is necessarily increasing in importance. Yet, though this new perspective will help the critical realist to understand his own age, it will not enable him to conceive the future *from the inside*.

In socialist realism, this barrier is removed. Since its ideological basis is an understanding of the future, individuals working for that future will necessarily be portrayed from the inside. Here is the first point of divergence, then, between critical and socialist realism. Socialist realism is able to portray from the inside human beings whose energies are devoted to the building of a different future, and whose psychological and moral make-up is determined by this. The great critical realists failed to break through this barrier—there are many instances of this failure, from Zola's Etienne Lantier to Martin du Gard's Jacques Tibault. The description of Jacques Tibault as a child, and as a young man, is masterly. There are, too, successful episodes dealing with Tibault's socialist phase—particularly the love scenes in the Paris of August 1914. But the task of portraying Tibault's new socialist consciousness was beyond Martin du Gard's powers.

The explanation is to be found in the *concrete* nature of the new socialist perspective. I should perhaps say here what I mean by 'concrete', since we shall be concerned with the problem of its realization later on. Concreteness, then, in my sense, involves an awareness of the development, structure and goal of society as a whole. The great critical realists did, of course, at times achieve a comprehensive description of the totality of society. Yet there was an important period in the history of critical realism (i.e. before Walter Scott) when the writer was hardly aware of the historical nature of the reality he described. And even nine-teenth-century historicism—which suffered a severe setback during the imperialist period—was deeply problematical. It was precisely where critical realism was most comprehensive and most profound—in the writings of Balzac and Tolstoy—that the historical diagnosis was most mistaken. Yet it permitted some extraordinary insights, both into man's social nature and into his role in history. The contrast was intensified in the imperialist period, following the decay of bourgeois historicism. Great realism was still possible—Thomas Mann is the obvious example—but it was at odds with its own ideology.

The perspective of socialism enables the writer to see society and history for what they are. This opens a fundamentally new, and highly fruitful, chapter in literary creation. Let us take two points. Socialist realism is a possibility rather than an actuality; and the effective realization of the possibility is a complex affair. A study of Marxism (not to speak of other activity in the

Socialist movement, even Party membership) is not of itself sufficient. A writer may acquire useful experience in this way, and become aware of certain intellectual and moral problems. But it is no easier to translate 'true consciousness' of reality into adequate aesthetic form than it is bourgeois 'false consciousness'.

Again, while it is true that a correct theoretical approach and a correct aesthetic (i.e. the creation of a typology) may often coincide, the methods and the results are not really identical. Their coincidence derives from the fact that both reflect the same reality. A correct aesthetic understanding of social and historical reality is the precondition of realism. A merely theoretical understanding—whether correct or incorrect—can only influence literature if completely absorbed and translated into suitable aesthetic categories. Whether the theory is correct or not is immaterial, since for a writer no theory, no conceptual understanding, can be more than a general guide. The relationship is indirect, dialectical; an erroneous, or partly erroneous, theory may nevertheless be a fruitful guiding principle. Lenin once remarked in a letter to Gorky, 'I am of the opinion that there is something in every philosophy which an artist can put to good use. . . .' And added, with Gorky's own work in mind, '. . . even if that philosophy be Idealistic'.

The reason is evidently that both approaches must grapple with the same infinite reality and endeavour to record their discoveries. Thus the most disparate approaches may yield fresh insights, and throw up new or hitherto neglected problems. Moreover, reality is neither static nor constant; the investigator cannot exhaust its substance. It is, on the contrary, a constant flux—only revealing a definite, though never simple, direction to the eye of the trained observer.

On the one hand, reality is forever throwing up new material, permitting older material to disappear from view. But the investigating subject, caught in its flux, is yet able to discover tendencies whose significance had not previously been understood. The development of new forms is intimately related to this active, unceasing exploration of reality. In this sense, there is certainly progress in art—although all works of art, whatever phase of development they belong to, are finally aesthetically equivalent. Schiller makes this point in his famous essay *Über Naive und Sentimentalische Dichtung*. Comparing the authors of Greek and modern literature—Shakespeare and Fielding are his examples—he concludes that the latter are superior in their treatment of women, and that this superiority reflects advances that have taken place in society. But he did not, of course, regard this as a criterion of higher aesthetic achievement.

A fuller understanding of the possibilities of human development, and of the laws underlying it, can form the basis of a new style—which in this sense, and only in this sense, will mark a higher stage in the development of art. Similarly, socialist perspective, correctly understood and applied, should enable the writer to depict life more comprehensively than any preceding perspective, not excluding that of critical realism.

To set out the points of contact and opposition between critical and socialist realism, I must recall our earlier discussion of the crisis of bourgeois literature. I need not refer to modernism in this place, since the opposition between it and socialist realism is evident. Earlier, we touched on an aspect of critical realism which served to illustrate the relation between it and socialist realism. I mean the role the revolutionary working class plays in modern society, without some account of which no picture of that society would be complete. I showed that critical realism was incapable of portraying this class and its problems from the inside. And I added that this was not the same thing as an inability to portray the past, and classes and groups existing in the past, from the inside.

Briefly, there are three possibilities. There is, first, the possibility of outright failure in an attempt to attack the new content directly (Roger Martin du Gard and, earlier, Zola). Secondly, there are cases where it has proved possible to evade the problem —Conrad, Sinclair Lewis—though the conditions which made this possible are rapidly disappearing (consider the difference between colonialism today and in Conrad's time; consider Louis Bromfield's attempt at a modern version of *Babbitt*). Or, thirdly, the problems of our time may be presented wholly within a bourgeois framework. The class struggle will be described from the bourgeois point of view, its effects on society being demonstrated only indirectly, by revealing the psychological and moral consequences. Thomas Mann is the great exponent of this method. Yet it is evident—and nobody was more conscious of this than Mann himself—that a literature accepting these presuppositions must be a literature of lowered vitality. It can never aspire to the richness and fullness of a Fielding or a Gottfried Keller; it will be the art of a society's old age. It will require hard work, deep thought, and profound imagination to achieve, in this roundabout way, the desired immediacy, to impose on shrinking and reluctant material a new and satisfactory wholeness.

Socialist realism is in a position, on the other hand, both to portray the totality of a society in its immediacy and to reveal its pattern of development. Of course, neither socialist realism nor critical realism are able to portray the totality of a society in the crude sense of the word. Even Balzac, who set out to do this in his *Comédie Humaine*, made this claim only in regard to the whole cycle. Each part, novel or short story, contains only a small segment, though complete in itself. But the greatness of his conception is that the whole is constantly present in the parts. Each individual novel is organically related to that whole; the various, immensely complex motivations, interrelations and combinations are embedded in an all-encompassing society. This ambition to portray a social whole, found in most great realists of the classical period, is inherited by socialist realism. Gorky's *Mother* does not offer a straightforward depiction of capitalism. Yet it would be wrong to compare this omission with, say, Mann's omission of the theme of class struggle from *Dr Faustus*. The latter presents only indirectly, through the career of one bourgeois intellectual, the life of the proletariat; whereas Gorky's novel, though it leaves out the bourgeoisie, focuses directly on the class struggle. Socialist realism, though it grapples with the same problems, is closer in its narrative method to the realism of the classical period, before realism was forced to adopt the indirect method of a Thomas Mann, than to the critical realism of our own time. Gorky, Sholokhov and others give proof of this.

Socialist realism's ambition to depict the totality of society is not, however, its specific stylistic criterion. It was not even that critical realism; even with Balzac there was the contrast between his grand conception and actual achievement. But socialist realism is certainly committed to the achievement of such totality more strongly than was critical realism. Not that the process of artistic realization is any less complex for that. In critical realism, as Zola's example shows, the ideal of a documentary totality, more suitable to the scientific monograph, was the product of certain inherent problems. I shall show that similar, and perhaps even greater, problems are inherent in socialist realism. The ideal of totality in art can never, of course, be more than a guiding principle, applied to a particular segment of life; it can never be more than an approximation to totality. Lenin demanded a similar dialectical conception of totality in regard to science: 'A problem can only be fully understood when all its aspects, all its implications, all its determinants, have been established and examined.' This demand applies even more to literature, where the achievement of depth, of intensive totality, always has priority over mere extensive totality.

From this it may appear that critical and socialist realism are virtually indistinguishable. But, in spite of the similarities, there are important qualitative differences. These derive from that hard-and-fast perspective of the future, that 'true consciousness', which socialist realism by definition possesses. This perspective enables the writer to obtain a fuller understanding of the life of the individual and of society than he could obtain elsewhere. Furthermore, a correct understanding of reality quickens the relation between theory and practice and gives rise to a new kind of human self-awareness: man becomes aware of his nature as an ineluctably social animal.

It is with the newness of this new content that we are concerned. New forms only result when such new phenomena enter human consciousness. Makarenko's *Didactic Poem* points to the unlimited formal possibilities inherent in the new content. In this respect, it is instructive to look at some of the best-known war novels. From *All Quiet on the Western Front* to *The Naked and the Dead* many honest, realistic novels of great aesthetic and ethical merit have been written. But war can only be understood in its totality if the writer has a perspective which enables him to understand the forces that lead to war, as Arnold Zweig had in *Education at Verdun* or A. Beck in *The Road to Volokamsk*. These latter works, far from giving us monographs on war, elevate the personal fate of their characters to the level of the typical; they mirror the totality of war in concrete relationships between typical, but living human beings.

Our account of the similarities between socialist and critical realism would be incomplete if the alliance between both these movements, and its historical necessity, were to be disregarded. The theoretical basis of this alliance is socialism's concern for the truth. In no other aesthetic does the truthful depiction of reality have so central a place as in Marxism. This is closely tied up with other elements in Marxist doctrine. For the Marxist, the road to socialism is identical with the movement of history itself. There is no phenomenon, objective or subjective, that has not its function in furthering, obstructing or deviating this development. A right understanding of such things is vital to the thinking socialist. Thus, *any* accurate account of reality is a contribution—whatever the author's subjective intention—to the Marxist critique of capitalism, and is a blow in the cause of socialism. In this sense, the alliance of socialism with realism may be said to have its roots in the revolutionary movement of the proletariat. A régime preparing for war, or a régime relying on oppression and confusion of the people, must necessarily

101

—as Mussolini, Hitler, and MacCarthy show—tend towards the suppression of realism.

But the alliance between critical and socialist realism is implicit also in the nature of art. It is impossible to work out the principles of socialist realism without taking into account the opposition between realism and modernism. In regard to the past, theoreticians of socialist realism are well aware of this; they have always considered the great critical realists allies in their struggle to establish the supremacy of realism in aesthetics. But the alliance is not merely theoretical. The historical insights in these writers' works, and the methods they used to achieve these insights, are vital to an understanding of the forces shaping the present and the future. They may help us to understand the struggle between the forces of progress and reaction, life and decay, in the modern world. To ignore all this is to throw away a most important weapon in our fight against the decadent literature of anti-realism. There were not a few modern critical realists, after all, who were allies of socialist realism in this fight—we have only to think of Romain Rolland.

Having established the existence of the alliance, we must show that the links between socialist realism and, say, Thomas Mann are not of a merely tactical kind; that socialist realism has a real claim to inherit the mantle of Goethe and Tolstoy. There are, of course, many examples of purely tactical collaboration. These came about frequently during the struggle against Fascism, and are to be found today again in the World Peace Movement. To apply the test of realism to these cases would be narrowly sectarian. Yet it is not easy to work out these distinctions in practice. Let us take the period between the wars, the period of Gide's and Malraux's short-lived left-wing sympathies. This alliance had no real ideological or aesthetic basis; it remained, consequently, no more than an episode. The World Peace Movement shows, again, that it is quite possible to distinguish between a writer's political stance and the character (realistic or otherwise) of his art. This is a point of some importance. Exaggerated claims were, of course, frequent at the time. During Gide's flirtation with socialism the

102

anti-realistic elements in his work were conveniently overlooked; then, after the break, his significance in contemporary literature was belittled. But this does not mean that a solution to the problem is theoretically impossible.

The alliance between socialist and critical realism rests on deeper-reaching ideological premisses. The most important is the proposition that socialist art is, of its nature, *national* art. I hasten to add that no sort of folk-mystique is implied in the phrase; still less any dogma about racial characteristics. It is just that any nation reflects the particular historical conditions through which it has passed. The decay of primitive communism took different forms in different places. Each European nation developed its own kind of feudalism. The decline of feudalism, the rise of capitalism, the particular structure of the working-class movement, however basically similar, differed importantly in different countries. An individual is born into a society that bears a specific physiognomy; his formative years are deeply influenced by its traditions; he is shaped by it as a thinking human being. And the great realist works of art are a main factor in creating the intellectual and spiritual climate which gives human personality its specifically national character. The stronger a writer's ties with the cultural heritage of his nation, the more original his work will be, even where he is in opposition to his own society and calls in a foreign tradition to redress the balance (Lessing and Shakespeare are a case in point. I have shown elsewhere how the influence of Tolstoy on Thomas Mann, Romain Rolland and Bernard Shaw helped to bring out specifically German, French and English characteristics in their writings.)

Today, critical and socialist realism are at one in their struggle against reactionary forces in politics and art. Lenin always insisted there was no Chinese Wall separating the bourgeois-democratic and proletarian revolutions. Equally, there is no such wall in the life of the individual, or in the community of writers. Gorky's development shows that the transition from a bourgeois-democratic view of the world to socialism may be gradual, almost intangible. Other bourgeois writers, such as Chekhov, display a similar pattern of transition, though Chekhov was never to cross the Rubicon. Thomas Mann was well aware of these transitional phases, experienced by the bourgeois writer who engages in self-criticism and glimpses the prospect of socialism on the horizon. In the twenties he wrote, in his *Paris Diary*: 'I am a bourgeois, certainly . . . yet to understand the condition of the bourgeoisie today does imply a detachment from it, an awareness of the new forces. It is foolish to mistake self-awareness for quietism. Nobody who knows himself intimately remains the same man.' However intangible the transition, there must be still a qualitative break. But the fact that such transitions are possible, and their manifest importance for the development of socialist realism, shows that the alliance is deep and intimate.

No analysis of socialist realism would be complete without a consideration of the reactionary, decadent elements in social and literary life which influenced it in its early stages. The evolution of Johannes R. Becher and Bertolt Brecht, or of Paul Eluard and Louis Aragon, into socialist writers would have been unthinkable without German Expressionism and French Surrealism. But the matter cannot be left at that. None of these writers would have developed 'automatically' from his modernist beginnings into a socialist writer (though he may well have been a socialist in politics all along), had not certain countervailing forces been operative. They drew much strength, of course, both from their personal experiences and from sources outside the life of their own country—one has only to think of the impact of the Russian Revolution and, later, of the building of socialism in the Soviet Union. But the fact remains that these writers drew, for the most part, on their own national literature—it is enough to point to the influence of Heine and Hölderlin on Becher's development as a socialist poet. There can be no doubt that traditional bourgeois realism is a useful ally for the socialist writer.

Nobody can dispute that this is so. But what of the relation between critical and socialist realism in the period *after* the seizure of power by the proletariat? We must bear in mind that, however violent the political break, people (including writers) will not be automatically transformed. Lenin once remarked that socialism had to be built by people who were moulded by capitalism. The truth is, people are only transformed when they participate in the transformation of reality. The progressive bourgeois realist must not be expected to embrace socialism the moment the proletariat seizes power. Some progressive intellectuals—even those who later on become socialists—may be driven into the opposite camp by the experience of class struggle in its acutest form. And the upheavals to which a revolution gives rise may cause serious doubts even among long-standing supporters of socialism (consider Gorky's reaction during the period of acute class struggle in Russia).

Conflicts of allegiance in literature are likely to be more complex than in the practical fields of politics and economics. Curiosity, a delight in novelty for novelty's sake, a romantic anticapitalism, may lead an extreme modernist to accept socialism. He may believe that his 'revolution of forms' is identical with socialist revolution, even its true expression. Again, sectarian communist intellectuals often fall for the dream of a 'proletarian culture', for the idea that a 'radically new' socialist culture can be produced, by artificial insemination as it were, independent of all traditions (*proletkult*). During the early years of the dictatorship of the proletariat in Russia such beliefs were rampant. The more level-headed communist theoreticians, Lenin in the lead, saw through these futile and basically anti-socialist ventures. But they could not be overcome before the new experience had been assimilated, before artists had understood the new forces at work in society and discovered how to give them artistic expression.

In view of this, it is not surprising that it took seventeen years —until after the 1st Congress of the Soviet Writers Union— for the term 'socialist realism' to become widely accepted. I will not describe in detail the preceding ideological discussion. The Congress's definition of the term (culminating in a famous paper read by Gorky) was the outcome of years of discussion between warring groups. The point of interest to us here is the new classification of 'fellow-traveller'. 'Fellow-travellers' are bourgeois writers, critical realists, who sympathize with, or at least acknowledge, the dictatorship of the proletariat and the goal of a socialist society. The term 'fellow-traveller' implies that the authorities of the time considered these writers allies in the making of a socialist literature. The decision was taken, I say, after many years of vehement discussion. The Central Committee resolution of 1925, acknowledging this alliance, was reversed by the RAPP group who acquired a dominating influence shortly afterwards. Soon, only 'explicitly' socialist writers were considered genuinely 'proletarian' (even Gorky and Sholokhov found themselves attacked). Only after the dissolution of RAPP in 1932 was the alliance re-affirmed, though there have been sporadic attempts since then to revive the RAPP ideology.

These ideological struggles in the Soviet Union illustrate our problem very well. But countries which became socialist later than the Soviet Union cannot simply adopt a formula of agreement reached after long and bitter ideological struggle. Lenin criticized again and again the sectarian assumption that the mass of the people could simply take over the intellectual vanguard's latest brainwave. In Lenin's view the masses can only be convinced of the truth of something when they have experienced it themselves. In this respect writers, too, belong to the masses, though they might not care to admit this. Literature depends on actual experience; resolutions, however well-meant, are no substitute for it. Soviet writers' experiences may shed light on the problem; but they do not provide a working model. The more so since, with the exception of China and Yugoslavia, none of the new socialist states owes its existence to civil war. In many respects, this development has its advantages. But there are also disadvantages. The shock-effect, the compulsion to make a decision which brings about a man's conversion, will be less pronounced in a mainly evolutionary process. Consequently, conversion presupposes more, not less political experience. I have not examined all the stumbling-blocks in the way of a bourgeois writer. But it is safe to conclude that many bourgeois writers, though sympathizing with socialism, will continue to work within the confines of critical realism.

Critical realism will therefore have a prolonged existence in the new socialist society. Some of the problems this raises we have dealt with already in a different context. First, there is that necessary precondition of critical realism even in capitalist society: not to reject the socialist perspective out of hand. This is still more necessary, of course, in socialist society. But here a dialectical shift is involved. As the perspective of socialism changes, as it is gradually translated into concrete reality, either the result will be growing approximation or, alternatively, a violent estrangement. Only a standstill is rare. Under socialism, the precarious balance familiar under capitalism gives way to more violent swings of the pendulum.

The second point concerns critical realism's inability to depict, from the inside, the social forces on which socialism is based. This is the case at present under capitalism. But it is far more critical for the writer who actually lives in a socialist society. Socialist reality confronts the critical realist with a society he is unable to describe from the inside. The fact that socialism is no longer a perspective, but has become the basis of his existence, makes it far more difficult for the bourgeois writer to evade the issue than it was for Thomas Mann. Is there, in fact, anything left for the critical realist to write about?

I would say: yes. We must not forget that remnants of the old order, and of the old consciousness, linger on and continue to inform many people's experience. But they do not survive—this is of crucial importance—in their old form. The character of any social phenomenon is determined by its orientation. A change of direction transforms not only the content and form of the phenomenon, it gives qualitatively new functions to that part of it which remains unchanged. Thus, the experiental material may seem familiar to the bourgeois writer; yet it has become, in fact, something altogether different. The writer is not simply called upon, as he was under capitalism, to relive, to re-explore historical change and development. He faces a quite new task: he must apply to his raw material the concrete perspective of socialism—which he once saw as an abstraction—in order that he may grasp the new realities in their actual novelty, and not as elements of disintegration or decay. To a certain extent, this process is possible within the limits of bourgeois consciousness; but it will tend to lead a writer to develop closer ties with socialism. There will thus be a large body of literature combining socialist and critical realism—a point to which we must return. But, in any case, it is important to appreciate the value of works still being written in the critical realist tradition. For it was typical of the sectarian, bureaucratic narrowness of the Stalinist period that, in describing socialist reality, the need for a socialist perspective was continually overstressed. Dogmatists even went so far as to deny to any but socialist writers the right to point out difficulties or criticize mistakes. And these difficulties or mistakes had to be remedied instantly in the piece of writing in question. It was Lenin who maintained that the rights of the working population had often to be safeguarded against the bureaucratic depredations of their superiors. There is much scope, in any case, for critical realism in the emerging socialist society. It is a society in process of transformation; and change is reflected in different ways in different social groups. The assessment of such changes depends on the character of the group's contribution to the development of society as a whole. We have examined, if only in general terms, why critical realism in periods of transition is socially justified and desirable. But since genuine Marxism (not the bureaucratized, subjectivized version of it) is based on the exploration of objective reality, it must be in the interests of Marxism to enter into a close alliance with critical realism.

Clearly, the complexity of the new subject-matter will demand a variety of new forms. It is sectarian to expect every criticism to be accompanied by a solution, or to be based exclusively on communist principles. This would lead to a severe reduction of the scope of critical realism in socialist society. Critical realism is important because it can describe the reaction of the non-socialist to the new society, can depict its transforming power, its rich inherent complexity. Critical realism has thus a significant contribution to make to present-day literature and is an important ally of emerging socialism.

Our discussion has been concerned chiefly with the presentation of contemporary social reality. But topics from the recent or remote past also appear in a new light, since the building of socialism alters the perspective of every past event. It is a matter not simply of reappraising familiar material but of revaluing the entire historical scene, as the new perspective throws light on previously neglected phenomena. This is not to say that a writer who clings to bourgeois values will be unable to write about such things. Far from it. If his view of the world makes allowances for a socialist perspective, he will certainly be able to do so. For, though understanding the past in terms of the new socialist reality may represent, qualitatively speaking, an advance, no total break with traditional perspectives is required. Critical realism can excel at this kind of elucidation of the past.

Let me repeat Heine's adage: socialism is the most effective way of fighting the forces the bourgeois writer has always fought. The enemy, in Heine's time, was German Chauvinism. Later, it was aggressive Imperialism; still later, Fascism. Today, it is the ideology of the Cold War and the preparation for nuclear war. The fight against the common enemy, which has led to close political alliances in our age, enables the critical realist to allow for the socialist perspective of history without relinquishing his own ideological position. The less his historical material is concerned with the building of socialism, the wider will be the critical realist writer's scope. Not that matters closely related to socialism are necessarily beyond the grasp of critical realism. Each socialist movement has a particular national character. There is a close connection between a people's achievement of nationhood and its decisive class struggles. This connection determines not only a nation's particular fate, but also the character of its bourgeois and proletarian revolutionary movements. The evaluation of this process is, of course, properly the object of Marxist historiography. But literature, too, furnishes valuable insights.

The character of the alliance between critical and socialist realism should now be clear. The fact that bourgeois and, later, proletarian revolutionary movements often defended national interests against the ruling classes (e.g. the peasant revolts in Germany and Hungary in the sixteenth century, or the French Revolution) has not been adequately investigated by historians. Nor has it, moreover, become a part of the historical consciousness of the socialist. Though bourgeois writers often underestimate the social factor, every insight of this sort contributes to the socialist understanding of history, and to the understanding of national characteristics. This is important because many socialist realists neglect the national character of class struggles, stressing only their social nature. Since critical realism tends to concentrate on these aspects—somewhat one-sidedly—it may prove a valuable ally, contributing new insights and correcting the no less one-sided approach of socialist realism. A good example is the Hungarian writer Gyula Illyes' *The Décza Tragedy*, which deals with the Hungarian peasants' revolt of 1514.

Then there is the question of the subjective experience of the individual writer. There can be no standstill in a writer's subjective development; to stand still, particularly in an age of crisis, is to retreat. I have pointed out the contradictions in the bourgeois intelligentsia's reaction to socialism. We have seen, too, that a purely negative reaction may put a writer out of touch with contemporary reality; it may reduce his perspective— rooted no longer in the present, but solely in the past—to a mere abstraction, and may prevent him imposing order on the human and social material at hand. The deeper the rift, the more tenuous will grow the links between the world as he sees it and objective reality, so that in the end he becomes alienated from what he should know most intimately. Such, often enough, is the fate of the emigré writer. So-called 'inner emigration' may be distinguished from emigration proper in that spiritual alienation is accompanied by social and political conformism and, frequently, by cynicism and hypocrisy. We have seen this to be the case with Gottfried Benn, Ernst Jünger and Ernst von Salomon (the fact that the mistakes, indeed crimes, committed in the Stalinist period seem to have confirmed points raised in this emigré literature, does not affect its position in the general historical development).

I have raised this more general sociological point in order to show up the essential contradictions inherent in any historical development. A writer's negative reaction to a historical pheno-menon may have many motives. His reaction may, of course, spring from inability to understand the new phase of social de-velopment. But it may also be the justified rejection of a reac-tionary phenomenon. The two things should not be confused. Admittedly, this kind of rejection and an inability to understand new developments may go together. Take Vercors' *Le Silence de la Mer*, set during the German occupation of France. Though Vercors' rejection may be abstract, his historical perspective is based on real events and springs from an objective historical de-velopment. It would not be difficult to find other illustrations.

The problem acquires a new dimension when we examine the opposition between reactionary and progressive positions. The 'inner' and 'outer' emigrés from socialism are bound to lose contact with historical reality, whereas the emigré writers of the anti-Fascist period profited from their opposition, learning to understand certain historical processes better than before their emigration. Arnold Zweig and Leon Feuchtwanger were good examples of this; as were, of course, Heinrich and Thomas Mann.

The problems here are manifold and complex, but not insol-uble. On the contrary, such conflicts can be extremely fruitful. In the transition period they form an important object of study: the relation of the bourgeois writer to socialist reality. It is strik-ing that both bourgeois and socialist literature have shown a preference for the autobiographical *Bildungsroman*. This is no coincidence. Both types of society are, unlike earlier societies, in a state of constant, dynamic change. An individual growing up in them has to work things out for himself and struggle for a place in the community. The young Marx pointed out that there is something arbitrary about the individual's class status under capitalism. The bourgeois or proletarian is not a bourgeois or proletarian by birth; he becomes a member of his class in the course of his personal development—unlike in feudal society where class status is neither freely chosen nor alterable. It is clear that this mobility is even more pronounced in socialist society, which is a melting-pot of many classes, some of which will ultimately disappear, others of which will undergo substantial reorientation before the classless society is established. In socialist society the individual will enjoy greater freedom to choose a place for himself in society than under capitalism ('freedom' being understood here, of course, as conscious acceptance of historical necessity—a necessity which subsumes much that is apparently arbitrary).

Having pointed to the similarities, we must now also point to the differences. We have seen why the *Bildungsroman* plays an important part in both literatures. Hegel once formulated—with a cynicism recalling that of Ricardo—the social purpose of education under capitalism as follows: 'During his years of apprenticeship the hero is permitted to sow his wild oats; he learns to subordinate his wishes and views to the interests of the society; he then enters that society's hierarchic scheme and finds in it a comfortable niche.' In one sense, many of the great bourgeois novels contradict Hegel; in another, they confirm him. They contradict him inasmuch as the educational process does not always culminate in acceptance of, and adaptation to, bourgeois society. The realization of youthful convictions and dreams is obstructed by the pressures of society; the rebellious hero is broken, and driven into isolation, but the reconciliation with society of which Hegel speaks is not always extracted. On the other hand, since the individual's conflict with society often ends in resignation, the end-effect is not so different from what Hegel suggests. For society emerges triumphant, in spite of the hero's struggles.

In socialist society, the situation is different. A *Bildungsroman*,

112

set in a socialist society, only apparently conforms to this pattern; experience itself will convert bourgeois individualist into social being. The end is not resignation. On the contrary, the process begins with resignation and leads on to active participation in the life of the community. Nor does the hero end up in isolation, as in so many of the later novels of critical realism. Rather, isolation gives way to an increasing involvement with the new social forces; a new and higher type of personality emerges. It is no accident that, whereas the typical bourgeois *Bildungsroman* takes its hero from childhood to the critical years of early adult life, its socialist counterpart often begins with the crisis of consciousness the adult bourgeois intellectual experiences when confronted with socialism. Both reflect reality. Under capitalism, we have to do with that element of arbitrariness which, as Marx showed, governs social existence. Under socialism, we have to do with the mental crisis which revolution represents for the bourgeois intellectual.

Particularly in the early phases of socialism, the main personal dilemma of the bourgeois intellectual—the decision for or against socialism—coincides with his dilemma as an artist. The coincidence can very well be stimulating. The energies released by his personal conflict with society strengthen his artistic efforts; whereas the correct formulation of his artistic problem may help the writer in his personal life. It is certainly striking how many novels of the early post-revolutionary period dealt with this crisis. It is even more striking that not a few writers were led to socialism through portraying this conflict, graduating from critical to socialist realism. The most interesting case is Alexei Tolstoy's powerful trilogy *Golgotha*, the first part of which was written in self-imposed exile, whereas the conclusion reflects a conscious acceptance of socialism. The same process can be observed in the writings of Fedin, Shaginyan and others.

During the transition period the dividing line between critical and socialist realism may not be drawn too rigidly. The two styles, distinguishable in theory, may well be found together in one work of art. This should not be surprising in the light of our

113

previous investigations. We saw that for critical realism under capitalism a socialist perspective can prove a fruitful stimulus. Clearly, with the growing currency of socialist ideas once a socialist society is established, this fruitful influence will increase—until, finally, the distinction between the two is blurred. This development will run parallel with the development of the new society. At first, the dictatorship of the proletariat introduces socialization only in limited fields; even there, people do not always respond at once to the new developments. The new socialist institutions, that is to say, have to rely for a considerable period on people who, mechanically obeying its formulas, retain a bourgeois mentality. In other spheres—for instance in agriculture—the transformation process is even slower. Not only do bourgeois forms of social life persist for a long time, but the new forms taking their place do not always correspond to a socialist pattern.

The transitional forms between critical and socialist realism thus have parallels in the development of socialism. The critical realist, following tradition, analyses the contradictions in the disintegrating old order and the emerging new order. But he does not only see them as contradictions in the outside world, he feels them to be contradictions within himself; though he tends—again following tradition—to emphasize the contradictions rather than the forces working towards reconciliation. The elucidation of these contradictions (often overlooked or neglected by socialist realism), and the significance accorded to them, serve to strengthen the alliance between the two types of realism. Both work with the same material, but they apply themselves in different ways to the exploration of social reality. The deeper they probe, the closer will social reality approximate to the desired socialist society, and the closer will grow the ties between critical and socialist realism. In the process, the negative perspective of critical realism will gradually be transformed into a positive, socialist perspective.

As socialism develops, critical realism, as a distinct literary style, will wither away. We have pointed out some of the limitations, and the problems, facing the critical realist in a socialist society. We have shown that the scope of critical realism will narrow as a society comes into being the portrayal of which is beyond the grasp of the critical realist. The critical realist will increasingly apply perspectives approximating to socialist realism. This will gradually lead to a withering-away of critical realism. The expression 'withering-away' can be taken quite literally. Society will eventually achieve a condition which only socialist realism can adequately describe. It will be a protracted process—more protracted than impatient sectarians maintain—but the outcome is inevitable. Critical realism will wither away, as the literary forms of feudalism have withered away. Of course, individual efforts may influence the process, speed it up or hinder it; but the process is ultimately determined by social developments alone. Neither government decrees nor literary manifestoes will be of assistance. Indeed, the opposite. The surviving remnants of capitalism in human consciousness and society are hardly to be eliminated by such means.

All this argues the superiority—historically speaking—of socialist realism (I cannot sufficiently emphasize that this superiority does not confer automatic success on each individual work of socialist realism). The reason for this superiority is the insights which socialist ideology, socialist perspective, make available to the writer: they enable him to give a more comprehensive and deeper account of man as a social being than any traditional ideology.

Let me repeat, we are dealing with a potentiality, the realization of which depends on prevailing circumstances. The emergence of a new style is dependent on many external influences; and there is also a double internal danger which, in the history of literature, has often marked periods of transition. There may be a reluctance, on the one hand, to accept the logic of some new subject-matter; there may be a timid hanging-on to traditional styles, an unwillingness to give up old habits. There may also be, on the other hand, a tendency to overemphasize *abstract* aspects of new subject-matter ('in history', wrote Hegel, 'every new phenomenon emerges first in abstract form'). Abstraction then gains the upper hand. Concrete realities—the exploration with the help of the new consciousness of as yet unexplored subject-matter will be neglected or considered of secondary importance. In bourgeois literature, Voltaire's tragedies illustrate the first of these conditions; the plays of Lillo or Diderot the second.

These dangers beset socialist realism too. What is more, they are to be found at its point of greatest strength, in its new, more concrete, more comprehensive perspective. In practice, lack of boldness in grappling with the new perspective is the less common problem, and theoretically the easier to resolve. Of course, there will always be writers who shy away from pursuing things to their logical conclusions, who fall back on received standards. The result will be a diluted, inferior version of bourgeois realism, lacking the virtues of that tradition. The literature likely to be taken as a model will be that of the later bourgeois period (*Zola, Neue Sachlichkeit*, the 'documentary' etc.) rather than that of the classical period of critical realism. It would be wrong to confuse this with the kind of critical realism which, as we showed earlier, is the process of transition towards socialist realism. The decisive factor, as in our earlier discussion of the relation between modernism and critical realism, is not the particular commitment, but the general orientation to which this commitment points. Actually, retrograde tendencies are surprisingly common, as the recurring emphasis on 'documentary' description in socialist realist writings shows.

The second danger—an exaggeration of perspective—seems to me of much greater significance. In an address to the IVth German Writers' Congress I examined some of the salient features of this phenomenon. I argued that the concrete character of perspective was all too often disregarded. Writers mistook developmental tendencies—really no more than guiding principles for the present—for blueprints of the future. I pointed out in my address the aesthetic consequences of this misunderstanding. But it is no less vital today to investigate the ideological reasons for

116

it; the more so since, in the light of the XXth Congress, the preceding period can now be seen in a clearer perspective. Although, where literature is concerned, many of the consequences have not yet been drawn.

I will start with what I consider the crucial question. In his last work on economics, Stalin sharply criticized that so-called 'economic subjectivism' which failed to see that socialist society, too, is determined by objective economic facts. Only the mastery of economic laws enables men to control their economic life. 'Economic subjectivism', however, attempts to apply those laws without regard to objective economic facts. Stalin here formulated a truth implicit in the Marxist classics. His attack on economic subjectivism was quite justified. But the tragic aspect of Stalin's career was that his own practice, and many of his pronouncements, helped to encourage economic subjectivism in the Soviet Union. The 'personality cult' was expressed often enough in Stalin's cavalier attitude to scientific facts and objective laws.

It is the method that concerns us here. In many cases Stalin's pronouncements may have corresponded with the truth; that is not our immediate concern. I wish to show that economic subjectivism was more than an accidental, short-lived aberration, corrected and criticized by Stalin in retrospect. Rather, it was the inevitable ideological consequence of the personality cult. In the field of economics the human will is confronted with hard facts. Ideology appears, on the other hand, a more pliable substance. And ideologies do prove, in fact, a good deal less obstinate than facts. Not only paper, in this respect, is patient—also stone: stone is indifferent to bad art as to good. The pliability is, of course, only apparent. Art too is governed by objective laws. An infringement of these laws may not have such practical consequences as do the infringement of economic laws; but it will result in work of inferior quality. Stalin's methods, therefore, met with much less resistance in the field of ideology than in the field of economics, where he often—shrewd as he was—gave in when resistance proved too strong. The natural sciences and technology were less vulnerable to the principles of economic

117

subjectivism than the social sciences and literature. In the latter a form of sectarianism arose which, though like that of earlier periods, was yet radically new. It will not do to trace back its origin to the *proletkult* and similar aberrations. We are confronted here with a phenomenon absolutely *sui generis*.

What were its essential features? I have pointed to the links with economic subjectivism. But there is a further point: if Marxist-Leninist objectivism is abandoned (though a nominal, subjectively sincere adherence to it may persist) the dialectical unity of theory and practice, of freedom and necessity, will be lost or dangerously weakened. The complex relationship between fundamental theory and everyday life, the day-to-day needs of political action, will be short-circuited.

The break-up of these mediating elements leads—in theory and in practice—to a false polarization. On the one hand, theory, from being a guide to practice, becomes a dogma, while, on the other hand, the element of contradiction between the two is eliminated. What we have is a polarization into dogmatism on the one hand, and pragmatism on the other. The former was widely discussed at the time of the XXth Congress. The latter has received rather less attention. It is nevertheless of great importance theoretically and practically. Marxism cannot be a guide to action if the relationship between perspective and actuality is subject to false simplification. But disregard for mediating elements leads to individual facts being seen without relation to the whole. Direct subsumption of facts under general, abstract principles will not alter this situation; for the transition between perspective and practice is then likely to be abrupt, and therefore unreal. And where facts are not distorted, but taken into due account, this is done in a pragmatic, and ultimately subjectivist, way.

Here again I shall confine myself to a general statement of the case: for we are concerned with the bearing of this theoretical constellation on literature. For literary purposes a correct, and not over-simplified, understanding of reality is clearly as vital as for pure theory. What the false polarization I have described

118

implies, in literary terms, is an inability to overcome naturalism. There are many varieties of naturalism. Common to all is the weakening of the relation between ideological principle and individual fact. That is why pragmatism and empiricism have an affinity with naturalism. In socialist realism, once the dictatorship of the proletariat has been established, such tendencies to naturalism assume a special character. Bourgeois naturalism expressed the bourgeois writer's bafflement, his inability to discover a rational pattern in the multiplicity of facts. In socialist naturalism the polarization into dogmatism and pragmatism is the decisive ideological factor (in bourgeois literature, too, 'the facts' were sometimes presented in the naturalist manner, without mediation, and related directly to abstract generalizations: Zola was an exponent of this naturalism, as were Upton Sinclair and the writers of *Neue Sachlichkeit*). This polarization had to result in a false aesthetics. The mistake lay in bringing Marxism too directly to bear on practical, day-to-day problems. Marxism thus became something abstract. Day-to-day problems and their tactical solution are, of course, part of a larger reality. In the writing of the Stalinist period, however, the real problems were overlooked and—as with economic subjectivism—the correctness of particular solutions became a matter for dogmatism. Literature ceased to reflect the dynamic contradictions of social life; it became the illustration of an abstract 'truth'. The aesthetic consequences of such an approach are all too evident. Even where this 'truth' was in fact true and not, as so often, a lie or a half-truth, the notion of literature-as-illustration was extremely detrimental to good writing.

The tendency to use literature as an illustration was paralleled by another fallacy. This involved a reversal of the correct relation between research, propaganda and agitation. Instead of basing propaganda on research, thus forging propaganda into a powerful instrument of agitation, agitation became the point of departure, the guiding principle of propaganda and research. Both were thus condemned to petrification and reduced in scope and effectiveness.

119

Agitation became, too, the regulative principle of literature. Of course, there has always been a type of literature passionately engaged in day-to-day political issues. It will, let us hope, continue to exist, and there is no reason why it should not aim at artistic perfection. But it is disastrous to subsume all literature under this head. Writers must be allowed to find their own point of contact with day-to-day politics, and be allowed to work out, as did Mayakovsky and Petöfi, suitable means of dealing with it. This is radically different from Stalinist literature-as-illustration, based on the requirements of agitation.

Let me take a specific example. The decisive distinction between socialism and all previous societies is that socialism aims to eliminate the antagonistic character of social contradictions. Literature has the immensely important task of describing this process, of exploring the problems thrown up by it, of showing how some traditional problems disappear and others are modified (I have dealt with these points elsewhere, particularly in my study of Makarenko). If, however, the elimination of this antagonistic character is seen as something immediately realizable, rather than as a process, both the antagonism and the contradiction, the motor of all development, will disappear from the reality to be depicted. That I am right in this is suggested by the fact that a few years ago official Soviet literary criticism launched an attack on the so-called 'drama-without-conflict'. Yet it was not only Soviet drama, but also Soviet novels, short stories and poetry that were emptied of conflict in that period.

This is not the only case in which dogmatic sectarianism in literature has come in for criticism. We have already cited Stalin's critique of economic subjectivism. But did these criticisms really get to the root of the problem? I think not. Though extreme cases of 'literature-without-conflict' were condemned, the doctrine of the priority of agitation over literature was adhered to. Now, in political life, the good agitator must be able to give an immediate answer to a question. But if he is prudent he will point out that the solutions to some problems require time. Many writers have lacked this prudence and literary

120

criticism has applauded them for it. Thus, a writer wishes to describe some problem in socialist society. But he also feels it to be his duty to offer a complete solution to the problem, within the framework of his work of art. There is, let us say, a speculator living in a certain village. He must be instantly converted or punished, it goes without saying. The fact that in an emergent socialist society there are still antagonistic contradictions is ignored by these writers. They do not see that the non-antagonistic character of contradictions only gradually prevails, and that even in the socialist society there may be insoluble conflicts. Nor do they see that neglect of existing contradictions —even if non-antagonistic in character—is liable precisely to render these contradictions antagonistic. What is involved is more than an impoverishment of literature in the face of the new reality. Since they fail to grasp the dialectical structure of these new non-antagonistic contradictions, their picture of the new reality will be distorted. Instead of a dialectical structure we shall get a static schematism. Here again, the new naturalism is rooted ideologically in Stalinism. Nor is it surprising that it should be found together with a false revolutionary romanticism.

This brings us to the distinction between a justified historical optimism—which can prove immensely fruitful—and that schematic optimism which gives rise to the 'happy ending'. I dealt with this problem in my study of Sholokhov's *Virgin Soil*, showing that many bourgeois critics' attacks on the optimism of socialist realism are due to an inability to understand the new developments. I pointed out that even where these attacks are justified, the 'happy ending' is qualitatively different from that in bourgeois literature. I examined the schematism common to both and pointed out the differences: 'These instances do not constitute a conscious falsification of social reality ... they represent an illegitimate simplification of its development. ... Historical optimism is degraded into a merely schematic optimism. The reader reacts to this with the same distaste as he does to a bourgeois "happy ending", though the method is not comparable.'

I have nothing to add to this formulation. Schematism was the consequence of an attitude that could not, so long as it predominated, be tackled by criticism of individual points—which was, indeed, never lacking and often correct in diagnosis.

Let us consider one or two concrete instances. Fadejev repeatedly—and, as I believe, rightly—pointed out that there were always superfluous characters in Soviet novels. This was certainly the case. What was the reason? It can be found, I believe, in the political and aesthetic situation produced by the dogmatism of the Stalinist period. If a writer feels obliged, like an agitator, to supply ready solutions to all the political problems of the day, his work will suffer. He will not be able, raising human conflicts to the level of the typical, to shed new light on the decisive problems of the age, as did Balzac or Tolstoy. For the complexity of such conflicts does not allow of the establishment of direct links between abstract principle and concrete fact. The writer analyses his problem theoretically and thinks up suitable characters to 'illustrate' it. The result is aesthetically disastrous. His composition consists of a pseudo-artistic superstructure resting on a pre-existent theory. Such work fails by the standards of realistic art, as Fadejev discovered. Many of the illustrative characters are gratuitous, irrelevant to the action—merely forming part of the theoretical conception. Failure was not due to lack of talent or artistic negligence—quite a few of these novels were the work of talented writers—but to misconceived artistic principles.

We have already touched on the problem of typology. What is the key to these 'typical' heroes of literature? The *typical* is not to be confused with the *average* (though there are cases where this holds true), nor with the *eccentric* (though the typical does as a rule go beyond the normal). A character is typical, in this technical sense, when his innermost being is determined by objective forces at work in society. Vautrin or Julien Sorel, superficially eccentric, are *typical* in their behaviour: the determining factors of a particular historical phase are found in them in concentrated form. Yet, though typical, they are never crudely 'illustrative'. There is a dialectic in these characters

122

linking the individual—and all accompanying accidentals—
with the typical. Levin was typical of the Russian land-owning
class at a period when everything was 'being turned upside
down'. The reader learns his personal peculiarities and is sometimes tempted to consider him, not wholly wrongly, as an out-
sider and an eccentric—until he realizes that such eccentricities
are the mark of an age in transition.

The heroes of that schematic literature I have described altogether lack these features. They are not typical, but topical.
Their features are prescribed by a specific political intention. I
should add that it is always extremely difficult to isolate 'typical'
features. The typical hero reacts with his entire personality to
the life of his age. Whenever socialist realism produces authentic
types—Fadejev's Levinson, or Sholokhov's Grigory Melyekov—
there is present this organic unity of profound individuality and
profound typicality. The characters produced by the schematists,
on the other hand, are both above and beneath the level of
typicality. The individual characterization is beneath it (whereas
Natasha Rostova's 'tripping step', say, or Anna Karenina's ball
costume are unquestionably typical), whereas what is intended
to establish their typicality may be irrelevant to their psychological make-up. This weakness is common, of course, to all
naturalistic literature—Zola's 'typical' characters have similar
shortcomings.

The same circumstances that produce these tendencies in
socialist realism also have other effects. What is socially typical,
and what is not? Economic subjectivism and sectarian dogmatism were guilty of the mechanical application of a political conception of the type in literature. In politics, the typical is in
opposition to the exceptional and the individual. In a particular
historical period one phenomenon can be represented by one
type only; the political character of the period is implicit in the
distinction between the type and the multiplicity of untypical
phenomena. In regard to the First World War, Lenin made this
distinction with decisive clarity; the war was the typical
product of imperialism. Criticizing those who maintained that

national wars were impossible in the age of imperialism, he stated that 'an age is the sum of many phenomena; it contains not only typical, but many other components'.

Art and literature, however, require a multiplicity of typical phenomena. The merest by-products of a phase of evolution may qualify as artistic types; this may be necessary for the work of art to be of lasting value. While in science (and politics) the typical and the untypical are strictly opposed, there is no authentic fictional character who is not typical in one way or another. What in nature is no more than an individual particularity may become typical in its literary presentation. The hierarchy of the compositional pattern gives a different, but no less truthful picture of reality than does natural science. That is why the dogmatic, mechanical application of political concepts in art must be dangerously restrictive. Particularly so if dogmatism, as in the Stalinist period, distorts reality by its subjectivist approach and expects the artist to adopt its own arbitrary typology. The use of this kind of typology is sufficient explanation of the rigidity and anaemia of socialist naturalism.

So far, we have concentrated on the drawbacks of this naturalism. In the nineteen-twenties, Franz Mehring, the German Marxist literary critic, showed in a perceptive study of German Naturalism how its shortcomings had led to its being supplemented by a special kind of romanticism. Indeed, one could say that romanticism (not the historical kind which arose at the beginning of the nineteenth century in reaction to the French Revolution, but the vague, generalized kind with which we have since become familiar) was the 'guilty conscience' of Naturalism. This formulation, of course, meets only the emotional and artistic side of the question. But it helps to account for the popularity of the slogan at different periods under very different conditions. It cannot, of course, explain the actual social origin of the tendency. We must now ourselves enquire into this, bearing in mind the importance of the emotional factor, the 'guilty conscience', for the dissemination of romantic attitudes.

We all know that 'revolutionary romanticism' has been, for

the last two decades, one of the hall-marks of socialist realism. How was it that romanticism—for all the attractiveness of the accompanying epithet—suddenly became part of Marxist aesthetics, although Marx and Lenin never used the term save with ironic contempt? To my mind, it has the same cause as Naturalism in socialist writing: the economic subjectivism and voluntarism produced by the personality cult. Revolutionary romanticism is the aesthetic equivalent of economic subjectivism.

The reasons are evident: economic subjectivism confuses what is subjectively desirable with what is objectively there. It reduces perspective, as we saw, to the level of practical day-to-day exigency. Life is thus robbed of its poetry. For the poetry of life lies in life's wholeness and self-sufficiency. This 'poetic' quality is inherent in all human development, in a man's individual fate, in growth and change. It reveals itself also in the 'slyness' of reality, of which Lenin used to speak—implying that the laws of existence are more complex than thought can easily express, and the realization of these laws a process so involved as to elude prediction. That profound awe in the face of experience we find in great minds—Leonardo or Lenin, Goethe or Tolstoy—is based on this knowledge. As is the enduring spell of all works of art that evoke life's inexhaustible dynamism.

Naturalism, socialist or otherwise, deprives life of its poetry, reduces all to prose. Naturalism's schematic methods are incapable of grasping the 'slyness' of reality, its wealth and beauty. That naturalism destroys the poetry of life is widely recognized, even by those critics and writers who have helped to bring about this state of affairs. Characteristically, public opinion in the socialist countries was never as vain of socialist naturalism as were bourgeois intellectuals of their modernism. But during the Stalinist period, as we know, many crucial Marxist doctrines were misrepresented. Literary theoreticians, therefore, thought up a poetical substitute for naturalism, 'revolutionary romanticism', instead of attempting an ideologically correct aesthetic solution.

Once again, the decisive error is the misconception of perspective, its equation with reality. This fallacy, which had produced the naturalistic de-poetization of reality in the first place, was now employed to turn back prose into poetry. To provide a theoretical basis, Marxism had to be interpreted voluntaristically, in the manner of economic subjectivism. According to Marx, the poetry of the socialist revolution cannot draw its inspiration from the past, as did that of the bourgeois revolution, but only from the future. Because of this orientation the proletarian revolution must, as Marx put it, practice permanent self-criticism of a thoroughness 'bordering on cruelty'. At the time of the Paris Commune, Marx formulated the duty of the revolutionary working-class as follows: 'This class is not concerned with putting ideals into practice. Its business is to bring to birth those new elements in the womb of decaying bourgeois society.' The poetry of the future demands, in Marx's eyes, sober and inexorable criticism of the forces leading—in actuality, not only in imagination—towards socialism. The poetry of the future is the means by which the character of the present can be understood in its own particularity. This notion of Marx is so clearly opposed to romanticism that further discussion may be dispensed with. It is not accidental that Marx should always have opposed romanticism and held Shakespeare and Balzac, the 'cruelly' critical realists, to be the masters of post-classical literature.

The theoreticians of revolutionary romanticism often refer to Lenin's saying, in his early work *What is to be done?*, that revolutionaries 'must dream'. Mistakenly. For Lenin always distinguished sharply between perspective and reality, even while pointing out their interdependence. He mocked the empiricists who got bogged down in day-to-day problems; who, like Eduard Bernstein, played off the 'ultimate goal' against the 'movement'. Lenin's 'dreaming' is simply that profound, passionate vision of a future which it is in the power of realistic revolutionary measures to construct. This 'dreaming' adds a new dimension to every revolutionary act, however insignificant. But only if that act is based on a correct understanding of objective reality, taking into account the complexity, the 'slyness' of reality. Lenin quotes some remarks of Pissarev's to the effect that dreaming is a healthy, life-enhancing activity—and uses them to make fun of his opponents. The true criterion of health, he says, is that the 'dreamer should observe life attentively, compare his observations with his phantasies, and devote his efforts diligently to the realization of his dreams'. Again, it is no accident that Lenin, like Marx, should regard Tolstoy's realism—in spite of its apparent ideological shortcomings—as a model for the literature of the future.

The 'dreams' of revolutionary romanticism are the direct opposite of what Lenin called for. Poetry, certainly, has the right to anticipate the future in imagination. Nor is this the exclusive privilege of lyrical poetry. In the works of revolutionary poets such 'dreaming' has always played an honourable role. But it is no less legitimate for characters in novels or plays to indulge in musing. Take the dream of young Nicolai Bolkonsky, which concludes Tolstoy's *War and Peace*. Its perspective is that of the Decembrist conspiracy of the eighteen-twenties, thus linking the novel with the progressive traditions of Russian history. Yet perspective and reality are carefully differentiated. The dream of Nicolai Bolkonsky can only afford us these glimpses of the future because we have already been introduced—through Pierre's Petersburg activities and his friends' reactions to them—to contemporary social movements. We must not forget that poetry also contains both components: description of reality and perspective. Poetry, to be successful, cannot feed on unfettered subjectivity. Its point of departure is life itself, and its particular mode of reflecting reality is governed by the same artistic laws as the novel and the drama. Where this structure is lacking, the poet's dreams disintegrate into those fragmentary perceptions of life, common, for instance, in German Expressionism. In contrast, the young Brecht's magnificent, hate-inspired 'Ballad of the Dead Soldier' draws its strength from a correct relationship between perspective and reality.

We have seen how economic subjectivism proved doubly fatal in the literary field. It limited, on the one hand, the portrayal of reality to a crude naturalism; and introduced, on the other, a false substitute in the shape of revolutionary romanticism. (I would like to mention, in this context, a point not directly related to our examination. The same tendencies led to a distortion of Lenin's concept of 'partisanship'. Lenin, in attacking Struve's notion of objectivism, showed that Marxism combines a profounder, richer objectivity with a conscious subjective 'partisanship'. Under Stalin objectivity was outlawed as 'objectivism', and its place taken by a wholly subjectivized 'partisanship'. The link with economic subjectivism is plain. It is plain, too, that this must lead to the erection of an insurmountable barrier between critical and socialist realism.)

A further factor was the particular kind of perspective employed. Stalin proclaimed two—erroneous and mutually exclusive—perspectives. First, there was the dogma that the class struggle would continue, and indeed gather momentum; the XXth Congress has succeeded in correcting this view. Stalin's second perspective was the dogma that communism, the second phase of socialism, was imminent. He tried to reconcile these two contradictory propositions by revising the Marxist doctrine of the withering-away of the state: communism would be brought about in spite of the capitalist encirclement of the only existing socialist state. The stage of 'from everyone according to his abilities, to everyone according to his needs' would be reached while the state, the political police and the rest were still in being.

The world of literature is concrete. A perspective of so heterogeneous and contradictory a nature is of no use to it. Indeed, the two components of this perspective were frequently applied separately, much to the detriment of the works in question, since it broke their unity. Stalin's dogma of the increasing violence of the class struggle led to a conspiracy theory of politics. The logical culmination was the Moscow purge trials, where all the contradictions of the developing Soviet system were blamed on the activities of spies and counter-revolutionaries. These monstrous violations of legality and elementary justice were based on grotesque reasoning. All the difficulties and conflicts that

123

arose during the building of socialism might have been avoided, according to this line of argument, if the security organs had done a better job and if Bukharin, Sinoviev, and the rest had been got rid of in 1917! In literature the adoption of this view led to a tedious schematism: difficulties in the building of socialism were invariably blamed on the activities of enemy agents. The exposure of these agents served as the denouement of the plot as well as the solution of the conflict. Both before the agent's arrival, and after his exposure, there existed an idyllic state of non-conflict. Naturally, there will be spies and counter-revolutionaries as long as two rival social systems exist. But these elements only use for their own criminal purposes existing difficulties, contradictions and mistakes. The perspective proclaimed by Stalin encouraged writers to attribute all evils to these 'enemies'. They were seen as not merely profiting from existing difficulties, but as actually creating them. It was in fact a deus-ex-machina solution—true to the spirit of the personality cult. Instead of the genuine tension underlying the struggle for socialism, we got the artificial tension of a detective story. Since these works relied on purely artificial effects, they were incapable of reflecting reality truthfully and were often extremely implausible. Their narrow, flat naturalistic psychology was then artifically enriched, and theoretically legitimated, by the introduction of revolutionary romanticism.

The perspective of imminent communism had a double effect on the psychological, moral, and typological structure of the novel. On the one hand, events which were still exceptional at that stage of socialism, were presented as typical. Thus, an otherwise interesting novel would be fatally marred by a scene in which a woman on a collective farm rejected the prize of a lamb she had herself brought up because communal is dearer to her heart than private property. Or a group of young Komsomols set out to win a harvest competition; they succeed in this by giving up their lunch-hour—only the strict orders of the supervisor can make them take some food and have a proper rest. The supervisor regards their zeal as an indication of the imminence of communism. Yet we are told that this collective farm is situated in a backward part of the country.

In criticizing revolutionary romanticism I am not concerned with the factual truth of such scenes. I only ask whether they can be considered 'typical'. From an artistic point of view, they are clearly not typical, as they are not presented as exceptional cases. They are presented as the average, the norm. But nor are they typical in the political sense of the word. They are there to illustrate an abstraction, the erroneous dogma of the imminence of communism. This is no more than wishful thinking; the characters and situations are not taken from life, they are abstract, bloodless, blurred. But the dogma of revolutionary romanticism claimed a higher reality for these false, untypical images of reality. Faulty theory may provide an excuse for these failures, but it will never make these works artistically convincing.

Lenin, and to a certain extent Stalin, considered it vital in the transitional period to awaken in the working population a personal interest in their work (by means of bonuses and differential pay). And one of the points in the XXth Congress' criticism of the past was that the socialist education of the population had been badly neglected. The 'typical' situation is, thus, that men have to be educated for socialism. Yet the literature we are criticizing abounds with types anticipating the imminent establishment of communism. Socialist consciousness is taken for granted; it is only a step to the achievement of communist consciousness. Of course, there may be genuine examples of this. At times these examples may even assume a symptomatic, and thus 'typical' significance. The periods of historical development are not, as in metaphysical speculation, to be rigidly distinguished. But it requires not only an increase in production so great that each can consume according to his needs (not according to his work, as in socialism) to achieve communism. There is also that new morality which, as Marx said, sees in work not just a means for ensuring the necessities of life, but 'one of the requirements of life itself'.

Naturally, this new attitude to work—and the increase in

130

production—will begin to take shape under socialism, and will gradually lead to communism. The emergence of characteristics anticipatory of the future may form the subject-matter of contemporary literature, and be presented as typical. But this is only possible if, as I showed in regard to naturalism, the specific ambience of such phenomena is conveyed. Here, the method used by Chernichevsky in his *What is to be done?* seems to me instructive. Chernichevsky's intention was to delineate the New Man. In Lopukhov, Kirsanov, Vera he confronts the reader with average representatives of the new reality who, basing their behaviour on a rational egotism, are out to overcome the contradictions inherent in the old order. On the other hand, there is the heroic figure of Rakhmetov, the revolutionary working for the overthrow of antiquated social institutions. Both are seen as types, and the typology is cleverly related in the writing to social and historical developments. Naturalism, as we have seen, cannot place its typology successfully in social reality. And revolutionary romanticism, by taking over the schematic, ahistorical typology of naturalism, is a substitute for poetry whose main effect is to accentuate the schematism of naturalism.

The notion that men should be given an incentive, a personal interest in their work, is no mere tactical device. It expresses the non-ascetic character of scientific socialism, in contrast to the asceticism of its primitive beginnings, and of its later sectarian aberrations. In the 1840's, the young Engels already saw the importance of this problem, examining it in a letter to Marx on the occasion of Max Stirner's newly published *The Individual and his Property*. Of interest to us is not so much Engels' brilliant refutation of Stirner's theory, but his vehement attack on Moses Hess who, in his ascetic Idealism, had minimized the role of egoism in social development and in socialist theory. In Engels' view, the only valid element in Stirner is his understanding of the role of egoism. Let me quote a crucial passage: 'What is valid is the idea that we have to make a cause our own before we are prepared to work for it, that, in this sense, apart from any hope of material gain, we are communists out of egoism, are human beings—and not merely individuals—out of egoism. ... If we take the living individual being as the basis, the starting-point for our image of the humanity, egoism—not Stirner's "rational egoism" alone, but our egoism of the heart—will be the ground of our love of humanity and give it sound roots.'

In every phase of socialist development, asceticism of one kind or another has made its appearance. As a phenomenon, it is contradictory. Its subjective motive may be of the noblest; its role, particularly in a revolutionary situation, may be admissible, indeed exemplary. Yet we cannot ignore the reactionary elements, in terms of socialist education, that it contains. That is why the ascetic attitude has been constantly criticized within the socialist movement. Examples in Soviet literature might be the 'ascetic' Nagulnov, criticized in Sholokhov's *Virgin Soil,* or the Levin criticized in Platonov's story *The Immortal Ones* (I refer the reader to a detailed analysis of this problem in my *Russian Realism and World Literature*). Another example is Julius Fucik, whose posthumous writings give evidence of an anti-ascetic heroism. And the same is true of many letters written by victims of Fascist terror.

It is important, in regard to the recent past, to see the problem of asceticism in proper perspective. Under 'bureaucratism', that typical by-product of Stalin's personality cult, asceticism acquired a special significance. It was imposed on the population by bureaucrats who were not inclined to adhere to it themselves. This aberration will no doubt disappear with the elimination of the personality cult and the establishment of socialist democracy.

The personal, 'egoistic' interest in work should be seen in a wider ideological context. It is really part of the struggle for the development of a full human personality—an indispensable element in it, as Lenin recognized. Revolutionary romanticism, by neglecting decisive facts as 'beneath its vision', (just as naturalism ignored them as 'above its vision'), contributed to that oversimplifying schematism which has distorted the actual grandeur of the spectacle of emergent socialism.

I must stress that my criticism is not directed towards all

socialist literature. Plainly, Gorky (in *Klim Samgin*), Sholokhov, Makarenko, Alexei Tolstoy, Trenov, Fedin, Anna Seghers, Tibor Dery and many others never fell into these errors. Certainly, the artistic greatness of a particular movement is always, and rightly, judged by its highest achievement; the merely average sinks into well-deserved oblivion. To discuss Elizabethan drama is to discuss Shakespeare, or at most a few of his major contemporaries, but not Middleton or Tourneur. To assess early nineteenth-century realism we have to concentrate on Balzac and Stendhal, not on those novelists who received equal, if not greater, attention at the time. Only if we bear this in mind, can we appreciate the epoch-making significance of socialist realism.

Socialist realism has still to fight to establish its international reputation. In the field of the arts, true coexistence, the exchange of ideas between representatives of different cultures, depends on mutual good-will. Discussion must concentrate on what is in common, however opposed the parties may otherwise be. This common basis, as far as socialist realism is concerned, is very slight. The blame for this rests mainly with the Cold War ideologists, who are out to discredit everything to do with socialism. But those theoreticians of modernism are also to blame for whom all literature must bear the stamp of decadent formalism. Slanderous attacks and misrepresentations can only, we should remember, be countered by an appeal to objective truth. And the truth about socialist realism is that its content and form were seriously distorted during the Stalinist period. It is necessary, therefore, not only to point out these artistic errors and their ideological origins, but to draw a strict line between genuine socialist realism and the works that suffer from these distortions.

It would be slanderous to assert that during the Stalinist period socialist democracy, or the socialist basis of economic construction, were totally destroyed. Yet the true face of socialism can only re-emerge if the forces working against it during past decades are eliminated. That, indeed, is one purpose of this investigation. To obtain recognition for the genuinely achieved successes of socialist realism, greater efforts must be made to distinguish between the distortions and the novel and constructive features.

What is the connection between our present analysis of these unfortunate developments in socialist realism and our previous discussion of the relationship between critical and socialist realism in a socialist society? The connection, I think, is very real. We have seen that naturalism and romanticism inhibited socialist writers' self-criticism in the face of socialist development. The 'slyness' of the contradictions it contains, its overcoming of internal and external opposition, its gradual progress towards the ultimate goal—all this was concealed by a superficial schematic subjectivism. Yet it was precisely the searching-out of contradictions, the revelation of history's labyrinthine course, that was the greatness of critical realism. That is why it can assist socialist realism in finding a cure for its self-inflicted wounds.

It must be said in justice that both socialist literature and socialist criticism have acknowledged this situation. There have always been those who recognized the aesthetic failings of much socialist realist writing, pointed to the mastery of the great critical realists of past and present, and recommended the study of their works to socialist writers. But this was a matter of instinct rather than of rational understanding. The superficial reasons for this mastery were seen, but the real reasons left unexplored. What was admired was often no more than technical proficiency or sophistication. I have tried to show that the reasons for this mastery of the great realists lie deeper than technical virtuosity. A writer's greatness springs from the depth and richness of his experience of reality. The study of the masters of past and contemporary critical realism will have to focus on the depth of these masters' experience; and the lessons learnt will be a subtler and more profound understanding of reality. Only then will the writer be in a position to develop his own talent, to seek the specific artistic form adequate to his specific content. This notion of literary mastery all the great realists have in common;

Goethe and Gorky have described in their autobiographies how this fruitful interrelation of life and literature comes into being.

I take this, then, to be the basis of any useful alliance between critical and socialist realism. The situation in the Soviet Union is different from that of societies which have more recently begun to move towards socialism. There, most of the critical realist writers have already adopted socialist realism. Socialist realism has produced a range of masterpieces, rooted in a socialist understanding of reality. For the Soviet writer, the alliance between critical and socialist realism has acquired the wider significance of a critical evaluation of the whole literary heritage. This need not prevent him, of course, from entering into an alliance with critical realists working in other socialist, or non-socialist countries.

The situation is different in the newer socialist states where there are still important representatives of critical realism. To tell the truth—and sincerity is the basis of any alliance—the sectarian schematism of the Stalinist period did much to alienate critical realist writers from socialism. Many socialist writers developed that 'communist arrogance', which Lenin so often attacked, that complacency which the ideological sectarianism and artistic narrowness of the Stalinist period supported and justified. In this atmosphere many critical realist writers stopped writing, or made concessions against their better judgment. And there were some writers, driven into opposition to socialism, whose artistic development was thereby seriously compromised.

The discussions which the XXth Congress has set going, and the profound changes these discussions have already brought in their train, will surely contribute to the break-up of dogmatism, and the establishment of a working alliance between critical and socialist realism. With the growth of socialist democracy, and the evolution towards genuinely national varieties of socialism, this alliance will deepen. The living traditions of critical realism have an important role to play in plotting the complex paths of socialist development.

SUMMER 1956.

WORLD PERSPECTIVES

What This Series Means

It is the thesis of *World Perspectives* that man is in the process of developing a new consciousness which, in spite of his apparent spiritual and moral captivity, can eventually lift the human race above and beyond the fear, ignorance, and isolation which beset it today. It is to this nascent consciousness, to this concept of man born out of a universe perceived through a fresh vision of reality, that *World Perspectives* is dedicated.

Man has entered a new era of evolutionary history, one in which rapid change is a dominant consequence. He is contending with a fundamental change, since he has intervened in the evolutionary process. He must now better appreciate this fact and then develop the wisdom to direct the process toward his fulfillment rather than toward his destruction. As he learns to apply his understanding of the physical world for practical purposes, he is, in reality, extending his innate capacity and augmenting his ability and his need to communicate as well as his ability to think and to create. And as a result, he is substituting a goal-directed evolutionary process in his struggle against environmental hardship for the slow, but effective, biological evolution which produced modern man through mutation and natural selection. By intelligent intervention in the evolutionary process man has greatly accelerated and greatly expanded the range of his possibilities. But he has not changed the basic fact that it remains a trial and error process, with the danger of taking paths that lead to sterility of mind and heart, moral apathy and intellectual inertia; and even producing social dinosaurs unfit to live in an evolving world.

Only those spiritual and intellectual leaders of our epoch who have a paternity in this extension of man's horizons are invited to participate in this Series: those who are aware of the truth that beyond the divisiveness among men there exists a primordial unitive power since we are all bound together by a common humanity more fundamental than any unity of dogma; those who recognize that the centrifugal force which has scattered and atomized mankind must be replaced by an integrating structure and process capable of bestowing meaning and purpose on existence; those who realize that science itself, when not inhibited by the limitations of its own methodology, when chastened and humbled, commits man to an indeterminate range of yet undreamed consequences that may flow from it.

Virtually all of our disciplines have relied on conceptions which are now incompatible with the Cartesian axiom, and with the static world view we once derived from it. For underlying the new ideas, including those of modern physics, is a unifying order, but it is not causality; it is purpose, and not the purpose of the universe and of man, but the purpose *in* the universe and *in* man. In other words, we seem to inhabit a world of dynamic process and structure. Therefore we need a calculus of potentiality rather than one of probability, a dialectic of polarity, one in which unity and diversity are redefined as simultaneous and necessary poles of the same essence.

Our situation is new. No civilization has previously had to face the challenge of scientific specialization, and our response must be new. Thus this Series is committed to ensure that the spiritual and moral needs of man as a human being and the scientific and intellectual resources at his command for *life* may be brought into a productive, meaningful and creative harmony.

In a certain sense we may say that man now has regained his former geocentric position in the universe. For a picture of the Earth has been made available from distant space, from the lunar desert, and the sheer isolation of the Earth has become plain. This is as new and as powerful an idea in history as any that has ever been born in man's consciousness. We are all becoming seriously concerned with our natural environment. And this concern is not only the result of the warnings given by biologists, ecologists and conservationists. Rather it is the result of a deepening awareness that something new has happened, that the planet Earth is a unique and precious place. Indeed, it may not be a mere coincidence that this awareness should have been born at the exact moment when man took his first step into outer space.

This Series endeavors to point to a reality of which scientific theory has revealed only one aspect. It is the commitment to this reality that lends universal intent to a scientist's most original and solitary thought. By acknowledging this frankly we shall restore science to the great family of human aspirations by which men hope to fulfill themselves in the world community as thinking and sentient beings. For our problem is to discover a principle of differentiation and yet relationship lucid enough to justify and to purify scientific, philosophic and all other knowledge, both discursive and intuitive, by accepting their interdependence. This is the crisis in consciousness made articulate through the crisis in science. This is the new awakening.

Each volume presents the thought and belief of its author and points to the way in which religion, philosophy, art, science, economics, politics and history may constitute that form of human activity which takes the fullest and most precise account of variousness, possibility, complexity and difficulty. Thus *World Perspectives* endeavors to define that ecumenical power of the mind and heart which enables man through his mysterious greatness to re-create his life.

This Series is committed to a re-examination of all those sides of human endeavor which the specialist was taught to believe he could safely leave aside. It attempts to show the structural kinship between subject and object; the indwelling of the one in the other. It interprets present and past events impinging on human life in our growing World Age and envisages what man may yet attain when summoned by an unbending inner necessity to the quest of what is most exalted in him. Its purpose is to offer new vistas in terms of world and human development while refusing to betray the intimate correlation between universality and individuality, dynamics and form, freedom and destiny. Each author deals with the increasing realization that spirit and nature are not separate and apart; that intuition and reason must regain their importance as the means of perceiving and fusing inner being with outer reality.

World Perspectives endeavors to show that the conception of wholeness, unity, organism is a higher and more concrete conception than that of matter and energy. Thus an enlarged meaning of life, of biology, not as it is revealed in the test tube of the laboratory but as it is experienced within the organism of life itself, is attempted in this Series. For the principle of life consists in the tension which connects spirit with the realm of matter, symbiotically joined. The element of life is dominant in the very texture of nature, thus rendering life, biology, a transempirical science. The laws of life have their origin beyond their mere physical manifestations and compel us to consider their spiritual source. In fact, the widening of the conceptual framework has not only served to restore order within the respective branches of knowledge, but has also disclosed analogies in man's position regarding the analysis and synthesis of experience in apparently separated domains of knowledge, suggesting the possibility of an ever more embracing objective description of the meaning of life.

Knowledge, it is shown in these books, no longer consists in a manipulation of man and nature as opposite forces, nor in the reduction of data to mere statistical order, but is a means of liberating mankind from the destructive power of fear, pointing the way toward the goal of the rehabilitation of the human will and the rebirth of faith and confidence in the human person. The works published also endeavor to reveal that the cry for patterns, systems and authorities is growing less insistent as the desire grows stronger in both East and West for the recovery of a dignity, integrity and self-realization which are the inalienable rights of man who may now guide change by means of conscious purpose in the light of rational experience.

The volumes in this Series endeavor to demonstrate that only in a society in which awareness of the problems of science exists can its discoveries start great waves of change in human culture, and in such a manner that these discoveries may deepen and not erode the sense of universal human community. The differences in the disciplines, their epistemological exclusiveness, the variety of historical experiences, the differences of traditions, of cultures, of languages, of the arts, should be protected and preserved. But the interrelationship and unity of the whole should at the same time be accepted.

The authors of *World Perspectives* are of course aware that the ultimate answers to the hopes and fears which pervade modern society rest on the moral fibre of man, and on the wisdom and responsibility of those who promote the course of its development. But moral decisions cannot dispense with an insight into the interplay of the objective elements which offer and limit the choices made. Therefore an understanding of what the issues are, though not a sufficient condition, is a necessary prerequisite for directing action toward constructive solutions.

Other vital questions explored relate to problems of international understanding as well as to problems dealing with prejudice and the resultant tensions and antagonisms. The growing perception and responsibility of our World Age point to the new reality that the individual person and the collective person supplement and integrate each other; that the thrall of totalitarianism of both left and right has been shaken in the universal desire to recapture the authority of truth and human totality. Mankind can finally place its trust not in a proletarian authoritarianism, not in a secularized humanism, both of which have betrayed the spiritual property right of history, but in a sacramental brotherhood and in the unity of knowledge. This new consciousness has created a widening of human horizons beyond every parochialism, and a revolution in human thought comparable to the basic assumption, among the ancient Greeks, of the sovereignty of reason; corresponding to the great effulgence of the moral conscience articulated by the Hebrew prophets; analogous to the fundamental assertions of Christianity; or to the beginning of the new scientific era, the era of the science of dynamics, the experimental foundations of which were laid by Galileo in the Renaissance.

An important effort of this Series is to re-examine the contradictory meanings and applications which are given today to such terms as democracy, freedom, justice, love, peace, brotherhood and God. The purpose of such inquiries is to clear the way for the foundation of a genuine *world* history not in terms of nation or race or culture but in terms of man in relation to God, to himself, his fellow man and the universe, that reach beyond immediate self-interest. For the meaning of the World Age consists in respecting man's hopes and dreams which lead to a deeper understanding of the basic values of all peoples.

World Perspectives is planned to gain insight into the meaning of man, who not only is determined by history but who also determines history. History is to be understood as concerned not only with the life of man on this planet but as including also such cosmic influences as interpenetrate our human world. This generation is discovering that history does not conform to the social optimism of modern civilization and that the organization of human communities and the establishment of freedom and peace are not only intellectual achievements but spiritual and moral achievements as well, demanding a cherishing of the wholeness of human personality, the "unmediated wholeness of feeling and thought," and constituting a never-ending challenge to man, emerging from the abyss of meaninglessness and suffering, to be renewed and replenished in the totality of his life.

Justice itself, which has been "in a state of pilgrimage and crucifixion" and now is being slowly liberated from the grip of social and political demonologies in the East as well as in the West, begins to question its own premises. The modern revolutionary movements which have challenged the sacred institutions of society by protesting social injustice in the name of social justice are here examined and re-evaluated.

In the light of this, we have no choice but to admit that the *un*-freedom against which freedom is measured must be retained with it, namely, that the aspect of truth out of which the night view appears to emerge, the darkness of our time, is as little abandonable as is man's subjective advance. Thus the two sources of man's consciousness are inseparable, not as dead but as living and complementary, an aspect of that "principle of complementarity" through which Niels Bohr has sought to unite the quantum and the wave, both of which constitute the very fabric of life's radiant energy.

There is in mankind today a counterforce to the sterility and danger of a quantitative, anonymous mass culture; a new, if sometimes imperceptible, spiritual sense of convergence toward human and world unity on the basis of the sacredness of each human person and respect for the plurality of cultures. There is a growing awareness that equality may not be evaluated in mere numerical terms but is proportionate and analogical in its reality. For when equality is equated with interchangeability, individuality is negated and the human person extinguished.

We stand at the brink of an age of a world in which human life presses forward to actualize new forms. The false separation of man and nature, of time and space, of freedom and security, is acknowledged, and we are faced with a new vision of man in his organic unity and of history offering a richness and diversity of quality and majesty of scope hitherto unprecedented. In relating the accumulated wisdom of man's spirit to the new reality of the World Age, in articulating its thought and belief, *World Perspectives* seeks to encourage a renaissance of hope in society and of pride in man's decision as to what his destiny will be.

World Perspectives is committed to the recognition that all great changes are preceded by a vigorous intellectual re-evaluation and reorganization. Our authors are aware that the sin of *hubris* may be avoided by showing that the creative process itself is not a free activity if by free we mean arbitrary, or unrelated to cosmic law. For the creative process in the human mind, the developmental process in organic nature and the basic laws of the inorganic realm may be but varied expressions of a universal formative process. Thus *World Perspectives* hopes to show that although the present apocalyptic period is one of exceptional tensions, there is also at work an exceptional movement toward a compensating unity which refuses to violate the ultimate moral power at work in the universe, that very power upon which all human effort must at last depend. In this way we may come to understand that there exists an inherent independence of spiritual and mental growth which, though conditioned by circumstances, is never determined by circumstances. In this way the great plethora of human knowledge may be correlated with an insight into the nature of human nature by being attuned to the wide and deep range of human thought and human experience.

Incoherence is the result of the present disintegrative processes in education. Thus the need for *World Perspectives* expresses itself in the recognition that natural and man-made ecological systems require as much study as isolated particles and elementary reactions. For there is a basic correlation of elements in nature as in man which cannot be separated, which compose each other and alter each other mutually. Thus we hope to widen appropriately our conceptual framework of reference. For our epistemological problem consists in our finding the proper balance between our lack of an all-embracing principle relevant to our way of evaluating life and in our power to express ourselves in a logically consistent manner.

Our Judaeo-Christian and Greco-Roman heritage, our Hellenic tradition, has compelled us to think in exclusive categories. But our *experience* challenges us to recognize a totality richer and far more complex than the average observer could have suspected—a totality which compels him to think in ways which the logic of dichotomies denies. We are summoned to revise fundamentally our ordinary ways of conceiving experience, and thus, by expanding our vision and by accepting those forms of thought which also include nonexclusive categories, the mind is then able to grasp what it was incapable of grasping or accepting before.

In spite of the infinite obligation of men and in spite of their finite power, in spite of the intransigence of nationalisms, and in spite of the homelessness of moral passions rendered ineffectual by the scientific outlook, beneath the apparent turmoil and upheaval of the present, and out of the transformations of this dynamic period with the unfolding of a world-consciousness, the purpose of *World Perspectives* is to help quicken the "unshaken heart of well-rounded truth" and interpret the significant elements of the World Age now taking shape out of the core of that undimmed continuity of the creative process which restores man to mankind while deepening and enhancing his communion with the universe.

RUTH NANDA ANSHEN

WORLD PERSPECTIVES

Volumes already published

I	APPROACHES TO GOD	Jacques Maritain
II	ACCENT ON FORM	Lancelot Law Whyte
III	SCOPE OF TOTAL ARCHITECTURE	Walter Gropius
IV	RECOVERY OF FAITH	Sarvepalli Radhakrishnan
V	WORLD INDIVISIBLE	Konrad Adenauer
VI	SOCIETY AND KNOWLEDGE	V. Gordon Childe
VII	THE TRANSFORMATIONS OF MAN	Lewis Mumford
VIII	MAN AND MATERIALISM	Fred Hoyle
IX	THE ART OF LOVING	Erich Fromm
X	DYNAMICS OF FAITH	Paul Tillich
XI	MATTER, MIND AND MAN	Edmund W. Sinnott
XII	MYSTICISM: CHRISTIAN AND BUDDHIST	Daisetz Teitaro Suzuki
XIII	MAN'S WESTERN QUEST	Denis de Rougemont
XIV	AMERICAN HUMANISM	Howard Mumford Jones
XV	THE MEETING OF LOVE AND KNOWLEDGE	Martin C. D'Arcy, S.J.
XVI	RICH LANDS AND POOR	Gunnar Myrdal
XVII	HINDUISM: ITS MEANING FOR THE LIBERATION OF THE SPIRIT	Swami Nikhilananda
XVIII	CAN PEOPLE LEARN TO LEARN?	Brock Chisholm
XIX	PHYSICS AND PHILOSOPHY	Werner Heisenberg
XX	ART AND REALITY	Joyce Cary
XXI	SIGMUND FREUD'S MISSION	Erich Fromm
XXII	MIRAGE OF HEALTH	René Dubos
XXIII	ISSUES OF FREEDOM	Herbert J. Muller
XXIV	HUMANISM	Moses Hadas
XXV	LIFE: ITS DIMENSIONS AND ITS BOUNDS	Robert M. MacIver

XXVI   CHALLEGE OF PSYCHICAL RESEARCH   Gardner Murphy

XXVII   ALFRED NORTH WHITEHEAD HIS REFLECTIONS
ON MAN AND NATURE   Ruth Nanda Anshen

XXVIII   THE AGE OF NATIONALISM   Hans Kohn

XXIX   VOICES OF MAN   Mario Pei

XXX   NEW PATHS IN BIOLOGY   Adolf Portmann

XXXI   MYTH AND REALITY   Mircea Eliade

XXXII   HISTORY AS ART AND AS SCIENCE   H. Stuart Hughes

XXXIII   REALISM IN OUR TIME   Georg Lukács

XXXIV   THE MEANING OF THE TWENTIETH CENTURY
Kenneth E. Boulding

XXXV   ON ECONOMIC KNOWLEDGE   Adolph Lowe

XXXVI   CALIBAN REBORN   Wilfrid Mellers

XXXVII   THROUGH THE VANISHING POINT
Marshall McLuhan and Harley Parker

XXXVIII   THE REVOLUTION OF HOPE   Erich Fromm

XXXIX   EMERGENCY EXIT   Ignazio Silone

XL   MARXISM AND THE EXISTENTIALISTS   Raymond Aron

XLI   PHYSICAL CONTROL OF THE MIND
José M. R. Delgado, M.D.

XLII   PHYSICS AND BEYOND   Werner Heisenberg

71 72 73 74   12 11 10 9 8 7 6 5 4 3 2 1

hARPER ✦ ᴛoRchbooks

American Studies: General

HENRY ADAMS Degradation of the Democratic Dogma. ‡ Introduction by Charles Hirschfeld. TB/1450

LOUIS D. BRANDEIS: Other People's Money, and How the Bankers Use It. Ed. with Intro, by Richard M. Abrams TB/3081

HENRY STEELE COMMAGER, Ed.: The Struggle for Racial Equality TB/1300

CARL N. DEGLER: Out of Our Past: The Forces that Shaped Modern America CN/2

CARL N. DEGLER, Ed.: Pivotal Interpretations of American History
Vol. I TB/1240; Vol. II TB/1241

A. S. EISENSTADT, Ed.: The Craft of American History: Selected Essays
Vol. I TB/1255; Vol. II TB/1256

LAWRENCE H. FUCHS, Ed.: American Ethnic Politics TB/1368

MARCUS LEE HANSEN: The Atlantic Migration: 1607-1860. Edited by Arthur M. Schlesinger. Introduction by Oscar Handlin TB/1052

MARCUS LEE HANSEN: The Immigrant in American History. Edited with a Foreword by Arthur M. Schlesinger TB/1120

ROBERT L. HEILBRONER: The Limits of American Capitalism TB/1305

JOHN HIGHAM, Ed.: The Reconstruction of American History TB/1068

ROBERT H. JACKSON: The Supreme Court in the American System of Government TB/1106

JOHN F. KENNEDY: A Nation of Immigrants. Illus. Revised and Enlarged. Introduction by Robert F. Kennedy TB/1118

LEONARD W. LEVY, Ed.: American Constitutional Law: Historical Essays TB/1285

LEONARD W. LEVY, Ed.: Judicial Review and the Supreme Court TB/1296

LEONARD W. LEVY: The Law of the Commonwealth and Chief Justice Shaw: The Evolution of American Law, 1830-1860 TB/1309

GORDON K. LEWIS: Puerto Rico: Freedom and Power in the Caribbean. Abridged edition TB/1371

HENRY F. MAY: Protestant Churches and Industrial America TB/1334

RICHARD B. MORRIS: Fair Trial: Fourteen Who Stood Accused, from Anne Hutchinson to Alger Hiss TB/1335

GUNNAR MYRDAL: An American Dilemma: The Negro Problem and Modern Democracy. Introduction by the Author.
Vol. I TB/1443; Vol. II TB/1444

GILBERT OSOFSKY, Ed.: The Burden of Race: A Documentary History of Negro-White Relations in America TB/1405

CONYERS READ, Ed.: The Constitution Reconsidered. Revised Edition. Preface by Richard B. Morris TB/1384

ARNOLD ROSE: The Negro in America: The Condensed Version of Gunnar Myrdal's An American Dilemma. Second Edition TB/3048

JOHN E. SMITH: Themes in American Philosophy: Purpose, Experience and Community TB/1466

WILLIAM R. TAYLOR: Cavalier and Yankee: The Old South and American National Character TB/1474

American Studies: Colonial

BERNARD BAILYN: The New England Merchants in the Seventeenth Century TB/1149

ROBERT E. BROWN: Middle-Class Democracy and Revolution in Massachusetts, 1691-1780. New Introduction by Author TB/1413

JOSEPH CHARLES: The Origins of the American Party System TB/1049

HENRY STEELE COMMAGER & ELMO GIORDANETTI, Eds.: Was America a Mistake? An Eighteenth Century Controversy TB/1329

WESLEY FRANK CRAVEN: The Colonies in Transition: 1660-1712† TB/3084

CHARLES GIBSON: Spain in America † TB/3077

CHARLES GIBSON, Ed.: The Spanish Tradition in America + HR/1351

LAWRENCE HENRY GIPSON: The Coming of the Revolution: 1763-1775 † Illus. TB/3007

JACK P. GREENE, Ed.: Great Britain and the American Colonies: 1606-1763. + Introduction by the Author HR/1477

AUBREY C. LAND, Ed.: Bases of the Plantation Society + HR/1429

JOHN LANKFORD, Ed.: Captain John Smith's America: Selections from his Writings † TB/3078

LEONARD W. LEVY: Freedom of Speech and Press in Early American History: Legacy of Suppression TB/1109

† The New American Nation Series, edited by Henry Steele Commager and Richard B. Morris.
‡ American Perspectives series, edited by Bernard Wishy and William E. Leuchtenburg.
α History of Europe series, edited by J. H. Plumb.
§ The Library of Religion and Culture, edited by Benjamin Nelson.
‖ Researches in the Social, Cultural, and Behavioral Sciences, edited by Benjamin Nelson.
Σ Harper Modern Science Series, edited by James A. Newman.
° Not for sale in Canada.
+ Documentary History of the United States series, edited by Richard B. Morris.
# Documentary History of Western Civilization series, edited by Eugene C. Black and Leonard W. Levy.
Λ The Economic History of the United States series, edited by Henry David et al.
¶ European Perspectives series, edited by Eugene C. Black.
** Contemporary Essays series, edited by Leonard W. Levy.
* The Stratum Series, edited by John Hale.

FERRY MILLER: Errand Into the Wilderness
TB/1139
FERRY MILLER & T. H. JOHNSON, Eds.: The Puritans: *A Sourcebook of Their Writings*
Vol. I TB/1093; Vol. II TB/1094
EDMUND S. MORGAN: The Puritan Family: *Religion and Domestic Relations in Seventeenth Century New England*
TB/1227
RICHARD B. MORRIS: Government and Labor in Early America
TB/1244
WALLACE NOTESTEIN: The English People on the Eve of Colonization: 1603-1630. † *Illus.*
TB/3006
FRANCIS PARKMAN: The Seven Years War: *A Narrative Taken from* Montcalm and Wolfe, The Conspiracy of Pontiac, *and* A Half-Century of Conflict. *Edited by John H. McCallum*
TB/3083
LOUIS B. WRIGHT: The Cultural Life of the American Colonies: 1607-1763. † *Illus.*
TB/3005
YVES F. ZOLTVANY, Ed.: The French Tradition in America +
HR/1425

American Studies: The Revolution to 1860

JOHN R. ALDEN: The American Revolution: 1775-1783. † *Illus.*
TB/3011
MAX BELOFF, Ed.: The Debate on the American Revolution, 1761-1783: *A Sourcebook*
TB/1225
RAY A. BILLINGTON: The Far Western Frontier: 1830-1860. † *Illus.*
TB/3012
STUART BRUCHEY: The Roots of American Economic Growth, 1607-1861: *An Essay in Social Causation. New Introduction by the Author.*
TB/1350
WHITNEY R. CROSS: The Burned-Over District: *The Social and Intellectual History of Enthusiastic Religion in Western New York, 1800-1850*
TB/1242
NOBLE E. CUNNINGHAM, JR., Ed.: The Early Republic, 1789-1828 +
HR/1394
GEORGE DANGERFIELD: The Awakening of American Nationalism, 1815-1828. † *Illus.*
TB/3061
CLEMENT EATON: The Freedom-of-Thought Struggle in the Old South. *Revised and Enlarged. Illus.*
TB/1150
CLEMENT EATON: The Growth of Southern Civilization, 1790-1860. † *Illus.*
TB/3040
ROBERT H. FERRELL, Ed.: Foundations of American Diplomacy, 1775-1872 +
HR/1393
LOUIS FILLER: The Crusade against Slavery: 1830-1860. † *Illus.*
TB/3029
DAVID H. FISCHER: The Revolution of American Conservatism: *The Federalist Party in the Era of Jeffersonian Democracy*
TB/1449
WILLIAM W. FREEHLING, Ed.: The Nullification Era: *A Documentary Record* ‡
TB/3079
WILLIM W. FREEHLING: Prelude to Civil War: *The Nullification Controversy in South Carolina, 1816-1836*
TB/1359
PAUL W. GATES: The Farmer's Age: *Agriculture, 1815-1860* △
TB/1398
FELIX GILBERT: The Beginnings of American Foreign Policy: *To the Farewell Address*
TB/1200
ALEXANDER HAMILTON: The Reports of Alexander Hamilton. ‡ *Edited by Jacob E. Cooke*
TB/3060
THOMAS JEFFERSON: Notes on the State of Virginia. ‡ *Edited by Thomas P. Abernethy*
TB/3052
FORREST MCDONALD, Ed.: Confederation and Constitution, 1781-1789 +
HR/1396

BERNARD MAYO: Myths and Men: *Patrick Henry, George Washington, Thomas Jefferson*
TB/1108
JOHN C. MILLER: Alexander Hamilton and the Growth of the New Nation
TB/3057
JOHN C. MILLER: The Federalist Era: 1789-1801. † *Illus.*
TB/3027
RICHARD B. MORRIS, Ed.: Alexander Hamilton and the Founding of the Nation. *New Introduction by the Editor*
TB/1448
RICHARD B. MORRIS: The American Revolution Reconsidered
TB/1363
CURTIS P. NETTELS: The Emergence of a National Economy, 1775-1815 △
TB/1438
DOUGLASS C. NORTH & ROBERT PAUL THOMAS, Eds.: *The Growth of the American Economy to 1860* +
HR/1352
R. B. NYE: The Cultural Life of the New Nation: 1776-1830. † *Illus.*
TB/3026
GILBERT OSOFSKY, Ed.: Puttin' On Ole Massa: *The Slave Narratives of Henry Bibb, William Wells Brown, and Solomon Northup* ‡
TB/1432
JAMES PARTON: The Presidency of Andrew Jackson. *From Volume III of the* Life of Andrew Jackson. *Ed. with Intro. by Robert V. Remini*
TB/3080
FRANCIS S. PHILBRICK: The Rise of the West, 1754-1830. † *Illus.*
TB/3067
MARSHALL SMELSER: The Democratic Republic, 1801-1815 †
TB/1406
TIMOTHY L. SMITH: Revivalism and Social Reform: *American Protestantism on the Eve of the Civil War*
TB/1229
JACK M. SOSIN, Ed.: The Opening of the West +
HR/1424
GEORGE ROGERS TAYLOR: The Transportation Revolution, 1815-1860 △
TB/1347
A. F. TYLER: Freedom's Ferment: *Phases of American Social History from the Revolution to the Outbreak of the Civil War. Illus.*
TB/1074
GLYNDON G. VAN DEUSEN: The Jacksonian Era: 1828-1848. † *Illus.*
TB/3028
LOUIS B. WRIGHT: Culture on the Moving Frontier
TB/1053

American Studies: The Civil War to 1900

W. R. BROCK: An American Crisis: *Congress and Reconstruction, 1865-67* °
TB/1283
T. C. COCHRAN & WILLIAM MILLER: The Age of Enterprise: *A Social History of Industrial America*
TB/1054
W. A. DUNNING: Reconstruction, Political and Economic: 1865-1877
TB/1073
HAROLD U. FAULKNER: Politics, Reform and Expansion: 1890-1900. † *Illus.*
TB/3020
GEORGE M. FREDRICKSON: The Inner Civil War: *Northern Intellectuals and the Crisis of the Union*
TB/1358
JOHN A. GARRATY: The New Commonwealth, 1877-1890 †
TB/1410
JOHN A. GARRATY, Ed.: The Transformation of American Society, 1870-1890 +
HR/1395
WILLIAM R. HUTCHISON, Ed.: American Protestant Thought: *The Liberal Era* ‡
TB/1385
HELEN HUNT JACKSON: A Century of Dishonor: *The Early Crusade for Indian Reform.* † *Edited by Andrew F. Rolle*
TB/3063
ALBERT D. KIRWAN: Revolt of the Rednecks: *Mississippi Politics, 1876-1925*
TB/1199
WILLIAM G. MCLOUGHLIN, Ed.: The American Evangelicals, 1800-1900: An Anthology ‡
TB/1382
ARTHUR MANN: Yankee Reforms in the Urban Age: *Social Reform in Boston, 1800-1900*
TB/1247

2

ARNOLD M. PAUL: Conservative Crisis and the Rule of Law: *Attitudes of Bar and Bench, 1887-1895. New Introduction by Author* TB/1415

JAMES S. PIKE: The Prostrate State: *South Carolina under Negro Government.* ‡ *Intro. by Robert F. Durden* TB/3085

WHITELAW REID: After the War: *A Tour of the Southern States, 1865-1866.* ‡ *Edited by C. Vann Woodward* TB/3066

FRED A. SHANNON: The Farmer's Last Frontier: ....*Agriculture, 1860-1897* TB/1348

VERNON LANE WHARTON: The Negro in Mississippi, 1865-1890 TB/1178

American Studies: The Twentieth Century

RICHARD M. ABRAMS, Ed.: The Issues of the Populist and Progressive Eras, 1892-1912 + HR/1428

RAY STANNARD BAKER: Following the Color Line: *American Negro Citizenship in Progressive Era.* ‡ *Edited by Dewey W. Grantham, Jr. Illus.* TB/3053

RANDOLPH S. BOURNE: War and the Intellectuals: *Collected Essays, 1915-1919.* ‡ *Edited by Carl Resek* TB/3043

A. RUSSELL BUCHANAN: The United States and World War II. † *Illus.*
Vol. I TB/3044; Vol. II TB/3045

THOMAS C. COCHRAN: The American Business System: *A Historical Perspective, 1900-1955* TB/1080

FOSTER RHEA DULLES: America's Rise to World Power: 1898-1954. † *Illus.* TB/3021

JEAN-BAPTISTE DUROSELLE: From Wilson to Roosevelt: *Foreign Policy of the United States, 1913-1945. Trans. by Nancy Lyman Roelker* TB/1370

HAROLD U. FAULKNER: The Decline of Laissez Faire, 1897-1917 TB/1397

JOHN D. HICKS: Republican Ascendancy: 1921-1933. † *Illus.* TB/3041

ROBERT HUNTER: Poverty: *Social Conscience in the Progressive Era.* ‡ *Edited by Peter d'A. Jones* TB/3065

WILLIAM E. LEUCHTENBURG: Franklin D. Roosevelt and the New Deal: 1932-1940. † *Illus.* TB/3025

WILLIAM E. LEUCHTENBURG, Ed.: The New Deal: *A Documentary History* + HR/1354

ARTHUR S. LINK: Woodrow Wilson and the Progressive Era: 1910-1917. † *Illus.* TB/3023

BROADUS MITCHELL: Depression Decade: *From New Era through New Deal, 1929-1941* ∧ TB/1439

GEORGE E. MOWRY: The Era of Theodore Roosevelt and the Birth of Modern America: 1900-1912. † *Illus.* TB/3022

WILLIAM PRESTON, JR.: Aliens and Dissenters: *Federal Suppression of Radicals, 1903-1933* TB/1287

WALTER RAUSCHENBUSCH: Christianity and the Social Crisis. ‡ *Edited by Robert D. Cross* TB/3059

GEORGE SOULE: Prosperity Decade: *From War to Depression, 1917-1929* ∧ TB/1349

GEORGE B. TINDALL, Ed.: A Populist Reader: *Selections from the Works of American Populist Leaders* TB/3069

TWELVE SOUTHERNERS: I'll Take My Stand: *The South and the Agrarian Tradition. Intro. by Louis D. Rubin, Jr.; Biographical Essays by Virginia Rock* TB/1072

Art, Art History, Aesthetics

CREIGHTON GILBERT, Ed.: Renaissance Art ** *Illus.* TB/1465

EMILE MALE: The Gothic Image: *Religious Art in France of the Thirteenth Century.* § 190 illus. TB/344

MILLARD MEISS: Painting in Florence and Siena After the Black Death: *The Arts, Religion and Society in the Mid-Fourteenth Century. 169 illus.* TB/1148

ERWIN PANOFSKY: Renaissance and Renascences in Western Art. *Illus.* TB/1447

ERWIN PANOFSKY: Studies in Iconology: *Humanistic Themes in the Art of the Renaissance. 180 illus.* TB/1077

JEAN SEZNEC: The Survival of the Pagan Gods: *The Mythological Tradition and Its Place in Renaissance Humanism and Art. 108 illus.* TB/2004

OTTO VON SIMSON: The Gothic Cathedral: *Origins of Gothic Architecture and the Medieval Concept of Order. 58 illus.* TB/2018

HEINRICH ZIMMER: Myths and Symbols in Indian Art and Civilization. *70 illus.* TB/2005

Asian Studies

WOLFGANG FRANKE: China and the West: *The Cultural Encounter, 13th to 20th Centuries. Trans. by R. A. Wilson* TB/1326

L. CARRINGTON GOODRICH: A Short History of the Chinese People. *Illus.* TB/3015

DAN N. JACOBS, Ed.: The New Communist Manifesto and Related Documents. *3rd revised edn.* TB/1078

DAN N. JACOBS & HANS H. BAERWALD, Eds.: Chinese Communism: *Selected Documents* TB/3031

BENJAMIN I. SCHWARTZ: Chinese Communism and the Rise of Mao T3/1308

BENJAMIN I. SCHWARTZ: In Search of Wealth and Power: *Yen Fu and the West* TB/1422

Economics & Economic History

C. E. BLACK: The Dynamics of Modernization: *A Study in Comparative History* TB/1321

STUART BRUCHEY: The Roots of American Economic Growth, 1607-1861: *An Essay in Social Causation. New Introduction by the Author.* TB/1350

GILBERT BURCK & EDITORS OF *Fortune:* The Computer Age: *And its Potential for Management* TB/1179

JOHN ELLIOTT CAIRNES: The Slave Power. ‡ *Edited with Introduction by Harold D. Woodman* TB/1433

SHEPARD B. CLOUGH, THOMAS MOODIE & CAROL MOODIE, Eds.: Economic History of Europe: *Twentieth Century* # HR/1388

THOMAS C.COCHRAN: The American Business System: *A Historical Perspective, 1900-1955* TB/1180

ROBERT A. DAHL & CHARLES E. LINDBLOM: Politics, Economics, and Welfare: *Planning and Politico-Economic Systems Resolved into Basic Social Processes* TB/3037

PETER F. DRUCKER: The New Society: *The Anatomy of Industrial Order* TB/1082

HAROLD U. FAULKNER: The Decline of Laissez Faire, 1897-1917 ∧ TB/1397

PAUL W. GATES: The Farmer's Age: *Agriculture, 1815-1860* ∧ TB/1398

WILLIAM GREENLEAF, Ed.: American Economic Development Since 1860 + HR/1353

J. L. & BARBARA HAMMOND: The Rise of Modern Industry. || *Introduction by R. M. Hartwell* TB/1417

ROBERT L. HEILBRONER: The Future as History: *The Historic Currents of Our Time and the Direction in Which They Are Taking America* TB/1386

ROBERT L. HEILBRONER: The Great Ascent: *The Struggle for Economic Development in Our Time* TB/3030

FRANK H. KNIGHT: The Economic Organization TB/1214

DAVID S. LANDES: Bankers and Pashas: *International Finance and Economic Imperialism in Egypt. New Preface by the Author* TB/1412

ROBERT LATOUCHE: The Birth of Western Economy: *Economic Aspects of the Dark Ages* TB/1290

ABBA P. LERNER: Everybody's Business: *A Reexamination of Current Assumptions in Economics and Public Policy* TB/3051

W. ARTHUR LEWIS: Economic Survey, 1919-1939 TB/1446

W. ARTHUR LEWIS: The Principles of Economic Planning. *New Introduction by the Author°* TB/1436

ROBERT GREEN MC CLOSKEY: American Conservatism in the Age of Enterprise TB/1137

PAUL MANTOUX: The Industrial Revolution in the Eighteenth Century: *An Outline of the Beginnings of the Modern Factory System in England°* TB/1079

WILLIAM MILLER, Ed.: Men in Business: *Essays on the Historical Role of the Entrepreneur* TB/1081

GUNNAR MYRDAL: An International Economy. *New Introduction by the Author* TB/1445

HERBERT A. SIMON: The Shape of Automation: *For Men and Management* TB/1245

PERRIN STRYER: The Character of the Executive: *Eleven Studies in Managerial Qualities* TB/1041

RICHARD S. WECKSTEIN, Ed.: Expansion of World Trade and the Growth of National Economies ** TB/1373

Education

JACQUES BARZUN: The House of Intellect TB/1051

RICHARD M. JONES, Ed.: Contemporary Educational Psychology: *Selected Readings* ** TB/1292

CLARK KERR: The Uses of the University TB/1264

Historiography and History of Ideas

HERSCHEL BAKER: The Image of Man: *A Study of the Idea of Human Dignity in Classical Antiquity, the Middle Ages, and the Renaissance* TB/1047

J. BRONOWSKI & BRUCE MAZLISH: The Western Intellectual Tradition: *From Leonardo to Hegel* TB/3001

EDMUND BURKE: On Revolution. Ed. by Robert A. Smith TB/1401

WILHELM DILTHEY: Pattern and Meaning in History: *Thoughts on History and Society.° Edited with an Intro. by H. P. Rickman* TB/1075

ALEXANDER GRAY: The Socialist Tradition: *Moses to Lenin °* TB/1375

J. H. HEXTER: More's Utopia: *The Biography of an Idea. Epilogue by the Author* TB/1195

H. STUART HUGHES: History as Art and as Science: *Twin Vistas on the Past* TB/1207

ARTHUR O. LOVEJOY: The Great Chain of Being: *A Study of the History of an Idea* TB/1009

JOSE ORTEGA Y GASSET: The Modern Theme. *Introduction by Jose Ferrater Mora* TB/1038

RICHARD H. POPKIN: The History of Scepticism from Erasmus to Descartes. *Revised Edition* TB/1391

G. J. RENIER: History: *Its Purpose and Method* TB/1209

MASSIMO SALVADORI, Ed.: Modern Socialism # HR/1374

GEORG SIMMEL et al.: Essays on Sociology, Philosophy and Aesthetics. *Edited by Kurt H. Wolff* TB/1234

BRUNO SNELL: The Discovery of the Mind: *The Greek Origins of European Thought* TB/1018

W. WARREN WAGER, ed.: European Intellectual History Since Darwin and Marx TB/1297

W. H. WALSH: Philosophy of History: In Introduction TB/1020

History: General

HANS KOHN: The Age of Nationalism: *The First Era of Global History* TB/1380

BERNARD LEWIS: The Arabs in History TB/1029

BERNARD LEWIS: The Middle East and the West ° TB/1274

History: Ancient

A. ANDREWS: The Greek Tyrants TB/1103

ERNST LUDWIG EHRLICH: A Concise History of Israel: *From the Earliest Times to the Destruction of the Temple in A.D. 70 °* TB/128

ADOLF ERMAN, Ed.: The Ancient Egyptians: *A Sourcebook of their Writings. New Introduction by William Kelly Simpson* TB/1233

THEODOR H. GASTER: Thespis: *Ritual Myth and Drama in the Ancient Near East* TB/1281

MICHAEL GRANT: Ancient History ° TB/1190

A. H. M. JONES, Ed.: A History of Rome through the Fifgth Century # Vol. I: *The Republic* HR/1364

Vol. II *The Empire:* HR/1460

SAMUEL NOAH KRAMER: Sumerian Mythology TB/1055

NAPHTALI LEWIS & MEYER REINHOLD, Eds.: Roman Civilization Vol. I: *The Republic* TB/1231

Vol. II: *The Empire* TB/1232

History: Medieval

MARSHALL W. BALDWIN, Ed.: Christianity Through the 13th Century # HR/1468

MARC BLOCH: Land and Work in Medieval Europe. *Translated by J. E. Anderson* TB/1452

HELEN CAM: England Before Elizabeth TB/1026

NORMAN COHN: The Pursuit of the Millennium: *Revolutionary Messianism in Medieval and Reformation Europe* TB/1037

G. G. COULTON: Medieval Village, Manor, and Monastery HR/1022

HEINRICH FICHTENAU: The Carolingian Empire: *The Age of Charlemagne. Translated with an Introduction by Peter Munz* TB/1142

GALBERT OF BRUGES: The Murder of Charles the Good: *A Contemporary Record of Revolutionary Change in 12th Century Flanders. Translated with an Introduction by James Bruce Ross* TB/1311

F. L. GANSHOF: Feudalism TB/1058

F. L. GANSHOF: The Middle Ages: *A History of International Relations. Translated by Rémy Hall* TB/1411

W. O. HASSALL, Ed.: Medieval England: *As Viewed by Contemporaries* TB/1205

DENYS HAY: The Medieval Centuries ° TB/1192

DAVID HERLIHY, Ed.: Medieval Culture and Socitey # HR/1340

4

J. M. HUSSEY: The Byzantine World TB/1057
ROBERT LATOUCHE: The Birth of Western Economy: *Economic Aspects of the Dark Ages* ° TB/1290
HENRY CHARLES LEA: The Inquisition of the Middle Ages. || *Introduction by Walter Ullmann* TB/1456
FERDINAND LOT: The End of the Ancient World and the Beginnings of the Middle Ages. *Introduction by Glanville Downey* TB/1044
H. R. LOYN: The Norman Conquest TB/1457
ACHILLE LUCHAIRE: Social France at the time of Philip Augustus. *Intro. by John W. Baldwin* TB/1314
GUIBERT DE NOGENT: Self and Society in Medieval France: *The Memoirs of Guibert de Nogent.* || *Edited by John F. Benton* TB/1471
MARSILIUS OF PADUA: The Defender of Peace. *The Defensor Pacis. Translated with an Introduction by Alan Gewirth* TB/1310
CHARLES PETET-DUTAILLIS: The Feudal Monarchy in France and England: *From the Tenth to the Thirteenth Century* ° TB/1165
STEVEN RUNCIMAN: A History of the Crusades Vol. I: *The First Crusade and the Foundation of the Kingdom of Jerusalem. Illus.* TB/1143
Vol. II: *The Kingdom of Jerusalem and the Frankish East 1100-1187. Illus.* TB/1243
Vol. III: *The Kingdom of Acre and the Later Crusades. Illus.* TB/1298
J. M. WALLACE-HADRILL: The Barbarian West: *The Early Middle Ages, A.D. 400-1000* TB/1061

History: Renaissance & Reformation

JACOB BURCKHARDT: The Civilization of the Renaissance in Italy. *Introduction by Benjamin Nelson and Charles Trinkaus. Illus.* Vol. I TB/40; Vol. II TB/41
JOHN CALVIN & JACOPO SADOLETO: A Reformation Debate. *Edited by John C. Olin* TB/1239
FEDERICO CHABOD: Machiavelli and the Renaissance TB/1193
THOMAS CROMWELL: Thomas Cromwell on Church and Commonwealth,: *Selected Letters 1523-1540.* ¶ *Ed. with an Intro. by Arthur J. Slavin* TB/1462
R. TREVOR DAVIES: The Golden Century of Spain, 1501-1621 ° TB/1194
J. H. ELLIOTT: Europe Divided; 1559-1598 *a* ° TB/1414
G. R. ELTON: Reformation Europe, 1517-1559 ° *a* TB/1270
DESIDERIUS ERASMUS: Christian Humanism and the Reformation: *Selected Writings. Edited and Translated by John C. Olin* TB/1166
DESIDERIUS ERASMUS: Erasmus and His Age: *Selected Letters. Edited with an Introduction by Hans J. Hillerbrand. Translated by Marcus A. Haworth* TB/1461
WALLACE K. FERGUSON et al.: Facets of the Renaissance TB/1098
WALLACE K. FERGUSON et al.: The Renaissance: *Six Essays. Illus.* TB/1084
FRANCESCO GUICCIARDINI: History of Florence. *Translated with an Introduction and Notes by Mario Domandi* TB/1470
WERNER L. GUNDERSHEIMER, Ed.: French Humanism, 1470-1600. * *Illus.* TB/1473
MARIE BOAS HALL, Ed.: Nature and Nature's Laws: *Documents of the Scientific Revolution* # HR/1420
HANS J. HILLERBRAND, Ed., The Protestant Reformation # HR/1342
JOHAN HUIZINGA: Erasmus and the Age of Reformation. *Illus.* TB/19

JOEL HURSTFIELD: The Elizabethan Nation TB/1312
JOEL HURSTFIELD, Ed.: The Reformation Crisis TB/1267
PAUL OSKAR KRISTELLER: Renaissance Thought: *The Classic, Scholastic, and Humanist Strains* TB/1048
PAUL OSKAR KRISTELLER Renaissance Thought II: *Papers on Humanism and the Arts* TB/1163
PAUL O. KRISTELLER & FHILIP P. WIENER, Eds.: Renaissance Essays TB/1392
DAVID LITTLE: Religion Order and Law: *A Study in Pre-Revolutionary England.* § *Preface by R. Bellah* TB/1418
NICCOLO MACHIAVELLI: History of Florence and of the Affairs of Italy: *From the Earliest Times to the Death of Lorenzo the Magnificent. Introduction by Felix Gilbert* TB/1027
ALFRED VON MARTIN: Sociology of the Renaissance. ° *Introduction by W. K. Ferguson* TB/1099
GARRETT MATTINGLY et al.: Renaissance Profiles. *Edited by J. H. Plumb* TB/1162
J. E. NEALE: The Age of Catherine de Medici ° TB/1085
J. H. PARRY: The Establishment of the European Hegemony: 1415-1715: *Trade and Exploration in the Age of the Renaissance* TB/1045
J. H. PARRY, Ed.: The European Reconnaissance: *Selected Documents* # HR/1345
BUONACCORSO PITTI & GREGORIO DATI: Two Memoirs of Renaissance Florence: *The Diaries of Buonaccorso Pitti and Gregorio Dati. Edited with Intro. by Gene Brucker. Trans. by Julia Martines* TB/1333
J. H. PLUMB: The Italian Renaissance: *A Concise Survey of Its History and Culture* TB/1161
A. F. POLLARD: Henry VIII. *Introduction by A. G. Dickens.* ° TB/1249
RICHARD H. POPKIN: The History of Scepticism from Erasmus to Descartes TB/139
PAOLO ROSSI: Philosophy, Technology, and the Arts, in the Early Modern Era 1400-1700. || *Edited by Benjamin Nelson. Translated by Salvator Attanasio* TB/1458
FERDINAND SCHEVILL: The Medici. *Illus.* TB/1010
FERDINAND SCHEVILL: Medieval and Renaissance Florence. *Illus.* Vol. I: *Medieval Florence* TB/1090
Vol. II: *The Coming of Humanism and the Age of the Medici* TB/1091
R. H. TAWNEY: The Agrarian Problem in the Sixteenth Century. *Intro. by Lawrence Stone* TB/1315
H. R. TREVOR-ROPER: The European Witch-craze of the Sixteenth and Seventeenth Centuries and Other Essays ° TB/1416
VESPASIANO: Renaissance Princes, Popes, and XVth Century: *The Vespasiano Memoirs. Introduction by Myron P. Gilmore. Illus.* TB/1111

History: Modern European

RENE ALBRECHT-CARRIE, Ed.: The Concert of Europe # HR/1341
MAX BELOFF: The Age of Absolutism, 1660-1815 TB/1062
OTTO VON BISMARCK: Reflections and Reminiscences. *Ed. with Intro. by Theodore S. Hamerow* ¶ TB/1357
EUGENE C. BLACK, Ed.: British Politics in the Nineteenth Century # HR/1427

5

EUGENE C. BLACK, Ed.: European Political History, 1815-1870: *Aspects of Liberalism* ¶ TB/1331

ASA BRIGGS: The Making of Modern England, 1783-1867: *The Age of Improvement* ° TB/1203

D. W. BROGAN: The Development of Modern France ° Vol. I: *From the Fall of the Empire to the Dreyfus Affair* TB/1184 Vol. II: *The Shadow of War, World War I, Between the Two Wars* TB/1185

ALAN BULLOCK: Hitler, A Study in Tyranny. ° *Revised Edition. Illus.* TB/1123

EDMUND BURKE: On Revolution. *Ed. by Robert A. Smith* TB/1401

E. R. CARR: International Relations Between the Two World Wars, 1919-1939 ° TB/1279

E. H. CARR: The Twenty Years' Crisis, 1919-1939: *An Introduction to the Study of International Relations* ° TB/1122

GORDON A. CRAIG: From Bismarck to Adenauer: *Aspects of German Statecraft. Revised Edition* TB/1171

LESTER G. CROCKER, Ed.: The Age of Enlightenment # HR/1423

DENIS DIDEROT: The Encyclopedia: *Selections. Edited and Translated with Introduction by Stephen Gendzier* TB/1299

JACQUES DROZ: Europe between Revolutions, 1815-1848. ° *a Trans. by Robert Baldick* TB/1346

JOHANN GOTTLIEB FICHTE: Addresses to the German Nation. *Ed. with Intro. by George A. Kelly* ¶ TB/1366

FRANKLIN L. FORD: Robe and Sword: *The Re-Louis XIV* TB/1217

ROBERT & ELBORG FORSTER, Eds.: European Society in the Eighteenth Century # HR/1404

C. C. GILLISPIE: Genesis and Geology: *The Decades before Darwin* § TB/51

ALBERT GOODWIN, Ed.: The European Nobility in the Enghteenth Century TB/1313

ALBERT GOODWIN: The French Revolution TB/1064

ALBERT GUERARD: France in the Classical Age: *The Life and Death of an Ideal* TB/1183

JOHN B. HALSTED, Ed.: Romanticism # HR/1387

J. H. HEXTER: Reappraisals in History: *New Views on History and Society in Early Modern Europe* ° TB/1100

STANLEY HOFFMANN et al.: In Search of France: *The Economy, Society and Political System In the Twentieth Century* TB/1219

H. STUART HUGHES: The Obstructed Path: *French Social Thought in the Years of Desperation* TB/1451

JOHAN HUIZINGA: Dutch Civilisation in the 17th Century and Other Essays TB/1453

LIONAL KOCHAN: The Struggle for Germany: *1914-45* TB/1304

HANS KOHN: The Mind of Germany: *The Education of a Nation* TB/1204

HANS KOHN, Ed.: The Mind of Modern Russia: *Historical and Political Thought of Russia's Great Age* TB/1065

WALTER LAQUEUR & GEORGE L. MOSSE, Eds.: Education and Social Structure in the 20th Century. ° *Volume 6 of the Journal* of Contemporary History TB/1339

WALTER LAQUEUR & GEORGE L. MOSSE, Ed.: International Fascism, 1920-1945. ° *Volume 1 of the* Journal of Contemporary History TB/1276

WALTER LAQUEUR & GEORGE L. MOSSE, Eds.: Literature and Politics in the 20th Century. ° *Volume 5 of the* Journal of Contemporary History. TB/1328

WALTER LAQUEUR & GEORGE L. MOSSE, Eds.: The New History: *Trends in Historical Research and Writing Since World War II.* ° *Volume 4 of the* Journal of Contemporary History TB/1327

WALTER LAQUEUR & GEORGE L. MOSSE, Eds.: 1914: *The Coming of the First World War.* ° *Volume3 of the* Journal of Contemporary History TB/1306

C. A. MACARTNEY, Ed.: The Habsburg and Hohenzollern Dynasties in the Seventeenth and Eighteenth Centuries # HR/1400

JOHN MCMANNERS: European History, 1789-1914: *Men, Machines and Freedom* TB/1419

PAUL MANTOUX: The Industrial Revolution in the Eighteenth Century: *An Outline of the Beginnings of the Modern Factory System in England* TB/1079

FRANK E. MANUEL: The Prophets of Paris: *Turgot, Condorcet, Saint-Simon, Fourier, and Comte* TB/1218

KINGSLEY MARTIN: French Liberal Thought in the Eighteenth Century: *A Study of Political Ideas from Bayle to Condorcet* TB/1114

NAPOLEON III: Napoleonic Ideas: *Des Idées Napoléoniennes, par le Prince Napoléon-Louis Bonaparte. Ed. by Brison D. Gooch* ¶ TB/1336

FRANZ NEUMANN: Behemoth: *The Structure and Practice of National Socialism, 1933-1944* TB/1289

DAVID OGG: Europe of the Ancien Régime, 1715-1783 ° *a* TB/1271

GEORGE RUDE: Revolutionary Europe, 1783-1815 ° *a* TB/1272

MASSIMO SALVADORI, Ed.: Modern Socialism # TB/1374

HUGH SETON-WATSON: Eastern Europe Between the Wars, 1918-1941 TB/1330

DENIS MACK SMITH, Ed.: The Making of Italy, 1796-1870 # HR/1356

ALBERT SOREL: Europe Under the Old Regime. *Translated by Francis H. Herrick* TB/1121

ROLAND N. STROMBERG, Ed.: Realism, Naturalism, and Symbolism: *Modes of Thought and Expression in Europe, 1848-1914* # HR/1355

A. J. P. TAYLOR: From Napoleon to Lenin: *Historical Essays* ° TB/1268

A. J. P. TAYLOR: The Habsburg Monarchy, 1809-1918: *A History of the Austrian Empire and Austria-Hungary* ° TB/1187

J. M. THOMPSON: European History, 1494-1789 TB/1431

DAVID THOMSON, Ed.: France: Empire and Republic, 1850-1940 # HR/1387

ALEXIS DE TOCQUEVILLE & GUSTAVE DE BEAUMONT: Tocqueville and Beaumont on Social Reform. *Ed. and trans. with Intro. by Seymour Drescher* TB/1343

G. M. TREVELYAN: British History in the Nineteenth Century and After: 1792-1919 ° TB/1251

H. R. TREVOR-ROPER: Historical Essays TB/1269

W. WARREN WAGAR, Ed.: Science, Faith, and MAN: *European Thought Since 1914* # HR/1362

MACK WALKER, Ed.: Metternich's Europe, 1813-1848 # HR/1361

ELIZABETH WISKEMANN: Europe of the Dictators, 1919-1945 ° *a* TB/1273

JOHN B. WOLF: France: 1814-1919: *The Rise of a Liberal-Democratic Society* TB/3019

Literature & Literary Criticism

JACQUES BARZUN: The House of Intellect TB/1051

6

W. J. BATE: From Classic to Romantic: *Premises of Taste in Eighteenth Century England* TB/1036

VAN WYCK BROOKS: Van Wyck Brooks: The Early Years: *A Selection from his Works, 1908-1921* Ed. with Intro. by Claire Sprague TB/3082

ERNST R. CURTIUS: European Literature and the Latin Middle Ages. *Trans. by Willard Trask* TB/2015

RICHMOND LATTIMORE, Translator: The Odyssey of Homer TB/1389

JOHN STUART MILL: On Bentham and Coleridge. *Introduction by F. R. Leavis* TB/1070

SAMUEL PEPYS: The Diary of Samual Pepys. ° *Edited by O. F. Morshead. 60 illus. by Ernest Shepard* TB/1007

ROBERT PREYER, Ed.: Victorian Literature ** TB/1302

ALBION W. TOURGEE: A Fool's Errand: *A Novel of the South during Reconstruction. Intro. by George Fredrickson* TB/3074

BASIL WILEY: Nineteenth Century Studies: *Coleridge to Matthew Arnold* ° TB/1261

RAYMOND WILLIAMS: Culture and Society, 1780-1950 ° TB/1252

Philosophy

HENRI BERGSON: Time and Free Will: *An Essay on the Immediate Data of Consciousness* ° TB/1021

LUDWIG BINSWANGER: Being-in-the-World: *Selected Papers. Trans. with Intro. by Jacob Needleman* TB/1365

H. J. BLACKHAM: Six Existentialist Thinkers: *Kierkegaard, Nietzsche, Jaspers, Marcel, Heidegger, Sartre* ° TB/1002

J. M. BOCHENSKI: The Methods of Contemporary Thought. *Trans. by Peter Caws* TB/1377

CRANE BRINTON: Nietzsche. *Preface, Bibliography, and Epilogue by the Author* TB/1197

ERNST CASSIRER: Rousseau, Kant and Goethe. *Intro. by Peter Gay* TB/1092

FREDERICK COPLESTON, S. J.: Medieval Philosophy TB/376

F. M. CORNFORD: From Religion to Philosophy: *A Study in the Origins of Western Speculation* § TB/20

WILFRID DESAN: The Tragic Finale: *An Essay on the Philosophy of Jean-Paul Sartre* TB/1030

MARVIN FARBER: The Aims of Phenomenology: *The Motives, Methods, and Impact of Husserl's Thought* TB/1291

MARVIN FARBER: Basic Issues of Philosophy: *Experience, Reality, and Human Values* TB/1344

MARVIN FARBER: Phenomenology and Existence: *Towards a Philosophy within Nature* TB/1295

PAUL FRIEDLANDER: Plato: *An Introduction* TB/2017

MICHAEL GELVEN: A Commentary on Heidegger's "Being and Time" TB/1464

J. GLENN GRAY: Hegel and Greek Thought TB/1409

W. K. C. GUTHRIE: The Greek Philosophers: *From Thales to Aristotle* ° TB/1008

G. W. F. HEGEL: On Art, Religion Philosophy: *Introductory Lectures to the Realm of Absolute Spirit.* || *Edited with an Introduction by J. Glenn Gray* TB/1463

G. W. F. HEGEL: Phenomenology of Mind. ° || *Introduction by George Lichtheim* TB/1303

MARTIN HEIDEGGER: Discourse on Thinking. *Translated with a Preface by John M. Anderson and E. Hans Freund. Introduction by John M. Anderson* TB/1459

F. H. HEINEMANN: Existentialism and the Modern Predicament TB/28

WERER HEISENBERG: Physics and Philosophy: *The Revolution in Modern Science. Intro. by F. S. C. Northrop* TB/549

EDMUND HUSSERL: Phenomenology and the Crisis of Philosophy. § *Translated with an Introduction by Quentin Lauer* TB/1170

IMMANUEL KANT: Groundwork of the Metaphysic of Morals. *Translated and Analyzed by H. J. Paton* TB/1159

IMMANUEL KANT: Lectures on Ethics. § *Introduction by Lewis White Beck* TB/105

WALTER KAUFMANN, Ed.: Religion From Tolstoy to Camus: *Basic Writings on Religious Truth and Morals* TB/123

QUENTIN LAUER: Phenomenology: *Its Genesis and Prospect. Preface by Aron Gurwitsch* TB/1169

MAURICE MANDELBAUM: The Problem of Historical Knowledge: *An Answer to Relativism* TB/1338

GEORGE A. MORGAN: What Nietzsche Means TB/1198

H. J. PATON: The Categorical Imperative: *A Study in Kant's Moral Philosophy* TB/1325

MICHAEL POLANYI: Personal Knowledge: *Towards a Post-Critical Philosophy* TB/1158

KARL R. POPPER: Conjectures and Refutations: *The Growth of Scientific Knowledge* TB/1376

WILLARD VAN ORMAN QUINE: Elementary Logic *Revised Edition* TB/577

WILLARD VAN ORMAN QUINE: From a Logical Point of View: *Logico-Philosophical Essays* TB/566

JOHN E. SMITH: Themes in American Philosophy: *Purpose, Experience and Community* TB/1466

MORTON WHITE: Foundations of Historical Knowledge TB/1440

WILHELM WINDELBAND: A History of Philosophy *Vol. I: Greek, Roman, Medieval* TB/38 *Vol. II: Renaissance, Enlightenment, Modern* TB/39

LUDWIG WITTGENSTEIN: The Blue and Brown Books ° TB/1211

LUDWIG WITTGENSTEIN: Notebooks, 1914-1916 TB/1441

Political Science & Government

C. E. BLACK: The Dynamics of Modernization: *A Study in Comparative History* TB/1321

KENNETH E. BOULDING: Conflict and Defense: *A General Theory of Action* TB/3024

DENIS W. BROGAN: Politics in America. *New Introduction by the Author* TB/1469

CRANE BRINTON: English Political Thought in the Nineteenth Century TB/1071

ROBERT CONQUEST: Power and Policy in the USSR: *The Study of Soviet Dynastics* ° TB/1307

ROBERT A. DAHL & CHARLES E. LINDBLOM: Politics, Economics, and Welfare: *Planning and Politico-Economic Systems Resolved into Basic Social Processes* TB/1277

HANS KOHN: Political Ideologies of the 20th Century TB/1277

ROY C. MACRIDIS, Ed.: Political Parties: *Contemporary Trends and Ideas* ** TB/1322

ROBERT GREEN MC CLOSKEY: American Conservatism in the Age of Enterprise, 1865-1910 TB/1137

MARSILIUS OF PADUA: The Defender of Peace. *The Defensor Pacis. Translated with an Introduction by Alan Gewirth* TB/1310

KINGSLEY MARTIN: French Liberal Thought in the Eighteenth Century: *A Study of Political Ideas from Bayle to Condorcet* TB/1114

BARRINGTON MOORE, JR.:Political Power and Social Theory: *Seven Studies* ‖ TB/1221
BARRINGTON MOORE, JR.: Soviet Politics—The Dilemma of Power: *The Role of Ideas in Social Change* ‖ TB/1222
BARRINGTON MOORE, JR.: Terror and Progress—USSR: *Some Sources of Change and Stability*
JOHN B. MORRALL: Political Thought in Medieval Times TB/1076
KARL R. POPPER: The Open Society and Its Enemies *Vol. I: The Spell of Plato* TB/1101 *Vol. II: The High Tide of Prophecy: Hegel, Marx, and the Aftermath* TB/1102
CONYERS READ, Ed.: The Constitution Reconsidered. *Revised Edition, Preface by Richard B. Morris* TB/1384
JOHN P. ROCHE, Ed.: Origins of American Political Thought: *Selected Readings* TB/1301
JOHN P. ROCHE, Ed.: American Political Thought: *From Jefferson to Progressivism* TB/1332
HENRI DE SAINT-SIMON: Social Organization, The Science of Man, and Other Writings. ‖ *Edited and Translated with an Introduction by Felix Markham* TB/1152
CHARLES SCHOTTLAND, Ed.: The Welfare State ** TB/1323
JOSEPH A. SCHUMPETER: Capitalism, Socialism and Democracy TB/3008
PETER WOLL, Ed.: Public Administration and Policy: *Selected Essays* TB/1284

Psychology

ALFRED ADLER: The Individual Psychology of Alfred Adler: *A Systematic Presentation in Selections from His Writings. Edited by Heinz L. & Rowena R. Ansbacher* TB/1154
ALFRED ADLER: Problems of Neurosis: *A Book of Case Histories. Introduction by Heinz L. Ansbacher* TB/1145
LUDWIG BINSWANGER: Being-in-the-World: *Selected Papers.* ‖ *Trans. with Intro. by Jacob Needleman* TB/1365
ARTHUR BURTON & ROBERT E. HARRIS: Clinical Studies of Personality *Vol. I* TB/3075 *Vol. II* TB/3076
HADLEY CANTRIL: The Invasion from Mars: *A Study in the Psychology of Panic* ‖ TB/1282
MIRCEA ELIADE: Cosmos and History: *The Myth of the Eternal Return* § TB/2050
MIRCEA ELIADE: Myth and Reality TB/1369
MIRCEA ELIADE: Myths, Dreams and Mysteries: *The Encounter Between Contemporary Faiths and Archaic Realities* § TB/1320
MIRCEA ELIADE: Rites and Symbols of Initiation: *The Mysteries of Birth and Rebirth* § TB/1236
HERBERT FINGARETTE: The Self in Transformation: *Psychoanalysis, Philosophy and the Life of the Spirit* ‖ TB/1177
SIGMUND FREUD: On Creativity and the Unconscious: *Papers on the Psychology of Art, Literature, Love, Religion.* § *Intro. by Benjamin Nelson* TB/45
J. GLENN GRAY: The Warriors: *Reflections on Men in Battle. Introduction by Hannah Arendt* TB/1294
WILLIAM JAMES: Psychology: *The Briefer Course. Edited with an Intro. by Gordon Allport* TB/1034
C. G. JUNG: Psychological Reflections. *Ed. by J. Jacobi* TB/2001
KARL MENNINGER, M.D.: Theory of Psychoanalytic Technique TB/1144
JOHN H. SCHAAR: Escape from Authority: *The Perspectives of Erich Fromm* TB/1155

MUZAFER SHERIF: The Psychology of Social Norms. *Introduction by Gardner Murphy* TB/3072
HELLMUT WILHELM: Change: *Eight Lectures on the I Ching* TB/2019

Religion: Ancient and Classical, Biblical and Judaic Traditions

W. F. ALBRIGHT: The Biblical Period from Abraham to Ezra TB/102
SALO W. BARON: Modern Nationalism and Religion TB/818
C. K. BARRETT, Ed.: The New Testament Background: *Selected Documents* TB/86
MARTIN BUBER: Eclipse of God: *Studies in the Relation Between Religion and Philosophy* TB/12
MARTIN BUBER: Hasidism and Modern Man. *Edited and Translated by Maurice Friedman* TB/839
MARTIN BUBER: The Knowledge of Man. *Edited with an Introduction by Maurice Friedman. Translated by Maurice Friedman and Ronald Gregor Smith* TB/135
MARTIN BUBER: Moses. *The Revelation and the Covenant* TB/837
MARTIN BUBER: The Origin and Meaning of Hasidism. *Edited and Translated by Maurice Friedman* TB/835
MARTIN BUBER: The Prophetic Faith TB/73
MARTIN BUBER: Two Types of Faith: *Interpenetration of Judaism and Christianity* ° TB/75
MALCOLM L. DIAMOND: Martin Buber: *Jewish Existentialist* TB/840
M. S. ENSLIN: Christian Beginnings TB/5
M. S. ENSLIN: The Literature of the Christian Movement TB/6
ERNST LUDWIG EHRLICH: A Concise History of Israel: *From the Earliest Times to the Destruction of the Temple in A.D. 70* ° TB/128
HENRI FRANKFORT: Ancient Egyptian Religion: *An Interpretation* TB/77
MAURICE S. FRIEDMAN: Martin Buber: *The Life of Dialogue* TB/64
ABRAHAM HESCHEL: The Earth Is the Lord's & The Sabbath. *Two Essays* TB/828
ABRAHAM HESCHEL: God in Search of Man: *A Philosophy of Judaism* TB/807
ABRAHAM HESCHEL: Man Is not Alone: *A Philosophy of Religion* TB/838
ABRAHAM HESCHEL: The Prophets: *An Introduction* TB/1421
T. J. MEEK: Hebrew Origins TB/69
JAMES MUILENBURG: The Way of Israel: *Biblical Faith and Ethics* TB/133
H. J. ROSE: Religion in Greece and Rome TB/55
H. H. ROWLEY: The Growth of the Old Testament TB/107
D. WINTON THOMAS, Ed.: Documents from Old Testament Times TB/85

Religion: General Christianity

ROLAND H. BAINTON: Christendom: *A Short History of Christianity and Its Impact on Western Civilization. Illus.* *Vol. I* TB/131; *Vol. II* TB/132
JOHN T. MCNEILL: Modern Christian Movements. *Revised Edition* TB/1402
ERNST TROELTSCH: The Social Teaching of the Christian Churches. *Intro. by H. Richard Niebuhr* *Vol.* TB/71; *Vol. II* TB/72

Religion: Early Christianity Through Reformation

ANSELM OF CANTERBURY: Truth, Freedom, and Evil: *Three Philosophical Dialogues. Edited and Translated by Jasper Hopkins and Herbert Richardson* TB/317

MARSHALL W. BALDWIN, Ed.: Christianity through the 13th Century # HR/1468

W. D. DAVIES: Paul and Rabbinic Judaism: *Some Rabbinic Elements in Pauline Theology. Revised Edition* ° TB/146

ADOLF DEISSMAN: Paul: *A Study in Social and Religious History* TB/15

JOHANNES ECKHART: Meister Eckhart: *A Modern Translation by R. Blakney* TB/8

EDGAR J. GOODSPEED: A Life of Jesus TB/1

ROBERT M. GRANT: Gnosticism and Early Christianity TB/136

WILLIAM HALLER: The Rise of Puritanism TB/22

GERHART B. LADNER: The Idea of Reform: *Its Impact on the Christian Thought and Action in the Age of the Fathers* TB/149

ARTHUR DARBY NOCK: Early Gentile Christianity and Its Hellenistic Background TB/111

ARTHUR DARBY NOCK: St. Paul ° TB/104

ORIGEN: On First Principles. *Edited by G. W. Butterworth. Introduction by Henri de Lubac* TB/311

GORDON RUPP: Luther's Progress to the Diet of Worms ° TB/120

Religion: The Protestant Tradition

KARL BARTH: Church Dogmatics: *A Selection. Intro. by H. Gollwitzer. Ed. by G. W. Bromiley* TB/95

KARL BARTH: Dogmatics in Outline TB/56

KARL BARTH: The Word of God and the Word of Man TB/13

HERBERT BRAUN, et al.: God and Christ: *Existence and Province. Volume 5 of Journal for Theology and the Church, edited by Robert W. Funk and Gerhard Ebeling* TB/255

WHITNEY R. CROSS: The Burned-Over District: *The Social and Intellectual History of Enthusiastic Religion in Western New York, 1800-1850* TB/1242

NELS F. S. FERRE: Swedish Contributions to Modern Theology. *New Chapter by William A. Johnson* TB/147

WILLIAM R. HUTCHISON, Ed.: American Protestant Thought: *The Liberal Era* ‡ TB/1385

ERNST KASEMANN, et al.: Distinctive Protestant and Catholic Themes Reconsidered. *Volume 3 of Journal for Theology and the Church, edited by Robert W. Funk and Gerhard Ebeling* TB/253

SOREN KIERKEGAARD: On Authority and Revelation: *The Book on Adler, or a Cycle of Ethico-Religious Essays. Introduction by F. Sontag* TB/139

SOREN KIERKEGAARD: Crisis in the Life of an Actress, *and Other Essays on Drama. Translated with an Introduction by Stephen Crites* TB/145

SOREN KIERKEGAARD: Edifying Discourses. *Edited with an Intro. by Paul Holmer* TB/32

SOREN KIERKEGAARD: The Journals of Kierkegaard. ° *Edited with an Intro. by Alexander Dru* TB/52

SOREN KIERKEGAARD: The Point of View for My Work as an Author: *A Report to History. § Preface by Benjamin Nelson* TB/88

SOREN KIERKEGAARD: The Present Age. § *Translated and edited by Alexander Dru. Introduction by Walter Kaufmann* TB/94

SOREN KIERKEGAARD: Purity of Heart. *Trans. by Douglas Steere* TB/4

SOREN KIERKEGAARD: Repetition: *An Essay in Experimental Psychology* § TB/117

SOREN KIERKEGAARD: Works of Love: *Some Christian Reflections in the Form of Discourses* TB/122

WILLIAM G MCLOUGHLIN, Ed.: The American Evangelicals: 1800-1900: *An Anthology* TB/1382

WOLFHART PANNENBERG, et al.: History and Hermeneutic. *Volume 4 of Journal for Theology and the Church, edited by Robert W. Funk and Gerhard Ebeling* TB/254

JAMES M ROBINSON, et al.: The Bultmann School of Biblical Interpretation: New Directions? *Volume 1 of Journal for Theology and the Church, edited by Robert W. Funk and Gerhard Ebeling* TB/251

F. SCHLEIERMACHER: The Christian Faith. *Introduction by Richard R. Niebuhr.* Vol. I TB/108; Vol. II TB/109

F. SCHLEIERMACHER: On Religion: Speeches to *Its Cultured Despisers. Intro. by Rudolf Otto* TB/36

TIMOTHY L. SMITH: Revivalism and Social Reform: *American Protestantism on the Eve of the Civil War* TB/1229

PAUL TILLICH: Dynamics of Faith TB/42

PAUL TILLICH: Morality and Beyond TB/142

EVELYN UNDERHILL: Worship TB/10

Religion: The Roman & Eastern Christian Traditions

A. ROBERT CAPONIGRI, Ed.: Modern Catholic Thinkers II: *The Church and the Political Order* TB/307

G. P. FEDOTOV: The Russian Religious Mind: *Kievan Christianity, the tenth to the thirteenth Centuries* TB/370

GABRIEL MARCEL: Being and Having: *An Existential Diary. Introduction by James Collins* TB/310

GABRIEL MARCEL: Homo Viator: *Introduction to a Metaphysic of Hope* TB/397

Religion: Oriental Religions

TOR ANDRAE: Mohammed: *The Man and His Faith* § TB/62

EDWARD CONZE: Buddhism: *Its Essence and Development.* ° *Foreword by Arthur Waley* TB/58

EDWARD CONZE: Buddhist Meditation TB/1442

EDWARD CONZE et al, Editors: Buddhist Texts through the Ages TB/113

ANANDA COOMARASWAMY: Buddha and the Gospel of Buddhism TB/119

H. G. CREEL: Confucius and the Chinese Way TB/63

FRANKLIN EDGERTON, Trans. & Ed.: The Bhagavad Gita TB/115

SWAMI NIKHILANANDA, Trans. & Ed.: The Upanishads TB/114

D. T. SUZUKI: On Indian Mahayana Buddhism. ° *Ed. with Intro. by Edward Conze.* TB/1403

Religion: Philosophy, Culture, and Society

NICOLAS BERDYAEV: The Destiny of Man TB/61

RUDOLF BULTMANN: History and Eschatology: *The Presence of Eternity* ° TB/91

RUDOLF BULTMANN AND FIVE CRITICS: Kerygma and Myth: *A Theological Debate* TB/80

RUDOLF BULTMANN and KARL KUNDSIN: Form Criticism: *Two Essays on New Testament Research. Trans. by F. C. Grant* TB/96
WILLIAM A. CLEBSCH & CHARLES R. JAEKLE: Pastoral Care in Historical Perspective: *An Essay with Exhibits* TB/148
FREDERICK FERRE: Language, Logic and God. *New Preface by the Author* TB/1407
LUDWIG FEUERBACH: The Essence of Christianity. § *Introduction by Karl Barth. Foreword by H. Richard Niebuhr* TB/11
C. C. GILLISPIE: Genesis and Geology: *The Decades before Darwin* § TB/51
ADOLF HARNACK: What Is Christianity? § *Introduction by Rudolf Bultmann* TB/17
KYLE HASELDEN: The Racial Problem in Christian Perspective TB/116
MARTIN HEIDEGGER: Discourse on Thinking. *Translated with a Preface by John M. Anderson and E. Hans Freund. Introduction by John M. Anderson* TB/1459
IMMANUEL KANT: Religion Within the Limits of Reason Alone. § *Introduction by Theodore M. Greene and John Silber* TB/FG
WALTER KAUFMANN, Ed.: Religion from Tolstoy to Camus: *Basic Writings on Religious Truth and Morals. Enlarged Edition* TB/123
JOHN MACQUARRIE: An Existentialist Theology: *A Comparison of Heidegger and Bultmann.* ° *Foreword by Rudolf Bultmann* TB/125
H. RICHARD NIERUHR: Christ and Culture TB/3
H. RICHARD NIEBUHR: The Kingdom of God in America TB/49
ANDERS NYGREN: Agape and Eros. *Translated by Philip S. Watson* ° TB/1430
JOHN H. RANDALL, JR.: The Meaning of Religion for Man. *Revised with New Intro. by the Author* TB/1379
WALTER RAUSCHENBUSCHS Christianity and the Social Crisis. ‡ *Edited by Robert D. Cross* TB/3059
JOACHIM WACH: Understanding and Believing. *Ed. with Intro. by Joseph M. Kitagawa* TB/1399

Science and Mathematics

JOHN TYLER BONNER: The Ideas of Biology. Σ *Illus.* TB/570
W. E. LE GROS CLARK: The Antecedents of Man: *An Introduction to the Evolution of the Primates.* ° *Illus.* TB/559
ROBERT E. COKER: Streams, Lakes, Ponds. *Illus.* TB/586
ROBERT E. COKER: This Great and Wide Sea: *An Introduction to Oceanography and Marine Biology. Illus.* TB/551
W. H. DOWDESWELL: Animal Ecology. *61 illus.* TB/543
C. V. DURELL: Readable Relativity. *Foreword by Freeman J. Dyson* TB/530
GEORGE GAMOW: Biography of Physics. Σ *Illus.* TB/567
F. K. HARE: The Restless Atmosphere TB/560
S. KORNER: The Philosophy of Mathematics: *An Introduction* TB/547
J. R. PIERCE: Symbols, Signals and Noise: *The Nature and Process of Communication* Σ TB/574
WILLÂRD VAN ORMAN QUINE: Mathematical Logic TB/558

Science: History

MARIE BOAS: The Scientific Renaissance, 1450-1630 ° TB/583
W. DAMPIER, Ed.: Readings in the Literature of Science. *Illus.* TB/512

STEPHEN TOULMIN & JUNE GOODFIELD: The Architecture of Matter: *The Physics, Chemistry and Physiology of Matter, Both Animate and Inanimate, as it has Evolved since the Beginnings of Science* TB/584
STEPHEN TOULMIN & JUNE GOODFIELD: The Discovery of Time TB/585
STEPHEN TOULMIN & JUNE GOODFIELD: The Fabric of the Heavens: *The Development of Astronomy and Dynamics* TB/579

Science: Philosophy

J. M. BOCHENSKI: The Methods of Contemporary Thought. *Tr. by Peter Caws* TB/1377
J. BRONOWSKI: Science and Human Values. *Revised and Enlarged. Illus.* TB/505
WERNER HEISENBERG: Physics and Philosophy: *The Revolution in Modern Science. Introduction by F. S. C. Northrop* TB/549
KARL R. POPPER: Conjectures and Refutations: *The Growth of Scientific Knowledge* TB/1376
KARL R. POPPER: The Logic of Scientific Discovery TB/576
STEPHEN TOULMIN: Foresight and Understanding: *An Enquiry into the Aims of Science. Foreword by Jacques Barzun* TB/564
STEPHEN TOULMIN: The Philosophy of Science: *An Introduction* TB/513

Sociology and Anthropology

REINHARD BENDIX: Work and Authority in Industry: *Ideologies of Management in the Course of Industrialization* TB/3035
BERNARD BERELSON, Ed., The Behavioral Sciences Today TB/1127
JOSEPH B. CASAGRANDE, Ed.: In the Company of Man: *Twenty Portraits of Anthropological Informants. Illus.* TB/3047
KENNETH B. CLARK: Dark Ghetto: *Dilemmas of Social Power. Foreword by Gunnar Myrdal* TB/1317
KENNETH CLARK & JEANNETTE HOPKINS: A Relevant War Against Poverty: *A Study of Community Action Programs and Observable Social Change* TB/1480
W. E. LE GROS CLARK: The Antecedents of Man: *An Introduction to the Evolution of the Primates.* ° *Illus.* TB/559
LEWIS COSER, Ed.: Political Sociology TB/1293
ROSE L. COSER, Ed.: Life Cycle and Achievement in America ** TB/1434
ALLISON DAVIS & JOHN DOLLARD: Children of Bondage: *The Personality Development of Negro Youth in the Urban South* ‖ TB/3049
ST. CLAIR DRAKE & HORACE R. CAYTON: Black Metropolis: *A Study of Negro Life in a Northern City. Introduction by Everett C. Hughes. Tables, maps, charts, and graphs* Vol. I TB/1086; Vol. II TB/1087
PETER E. DRUCKER: The New Society: *The Anatomy of Industrial Order* TB/1082
CORA DU BOIS: The People of Alor. *With a Preface by the Author* Vol. I *Illus.* TB/1042; Vol. II TB/1043
EMILE DURKHEIM et al.: Essays on Sociology and Philosophy: *with Appraisals of Durkheim's Life and Thought.* ‖ *Edited by Kurt H. Wolff* TB/1151
LEON FESTINGER, HENRY W. RIECKEN, STANLEY SCHACHTER: When Prophecy Fails: *A Social and Psychological Study of a Modern Group that Predicted the Destruction of the World* ‖ TB/1132

CHARLES Y. GLOCK & RODNEY STARK: Christian Beliefs and Anti-Semitism. *Introduction by the Authors* TB/1454

ALVIN W. GOULDNER: The Hellenic World TB/1479

ALVIN W. GOULDNER: Wildcat Strike: *A Study in Worker-Management Relationships* || TB/1176

CESAR GRANA: Modernity and Its Discontents: *French Society and the French Man of Letters in the Nineteenth Century* TB/1318

L. S. B. LEAKEY: Adam's Ancestors: *The Evolution of Man and His Culture. Illus.* TB/1019

KURT LEWIN: Field Theory in Social Science: *Selected Theoretical Papers.* || *Edited by Dorwin Cartwright* TB/1135

RITCHIE P. LOWRY: Who's Running This Town? *Community Leadership and Social Change* TB/1383

R. M. MACIVER: Social Causation TB/1153

GARY T. MARX: Protest and Prejudice: *A Study of Belief in the Black Community* TB/1435

ROBERT K. MERTON, LEONARD AND BROOM, LEONARD S. COTTRELL, JR., Editors: Sociology Today: *Problems and Prospects* || Vol. I TB/1173; Vol. II TB/1174

GILBERT OSOFSKY, Ed.: The Burden of Race: A *Documentary History of Negro-White Relations in America* TB/1405

GILBERT OSOFSKY: Harlem: The Making of a Ghetto: *Negro New York 1890-1930* TB/1381

TALCOTT PARSONS & EDWARD A. SHILS, Editors: Toward a General Theory of Action: *Theoretical Foundations for the Social Sciences* TB/1083

PHILIP RIEFF: The Triumph of the Therapeutic: *Uses of Faith After Freud* TB/1360

JOHN H. ROHRER & MUNRO S. EDMONSON, Eds.: The Eighth Generation Grows Up: *Cultures and Personalities of New Orleans Negroes* || TB/3050

ARNOLD ROSE: The Negro in America: *The Condensed Version of Gunnar Myrdal's* An American Dilemma. *Second Edition* TB/3048

GEORGE ROSEN: Madness in Society: *Chapters in the Historical Sociology of Mental Illness.* || *Preface by Benjamin Nelson* TB/1337

PHILIP SELZNICK: TVA and the Grass Roots: *A Study in the Sociology of Formal Organization* TB/1230

PITIRIM A. SOROKIN: Contemporary Sociological Theories: *Through the First Quarter of the Twentieth Century* TB/3046

MAURICE R. STEIN: The Eclipse of Community: *An Interpretation of American Studies* TB/1128

WILLIAM I. THOMAS: The Unadjusted Girl: *With Cases and Standpoint for Behavior Analysis. Intro. by Michael Parenti* TB/1319

EDWARD A. TIRYAKIAN, Ed.: Sociological Theory, Values and Sociocultural Change: *Essays in Honor of Pitirim A. Sorokin* ° TB/1316

FERDINAND TONNIES: Community and Society: *Gemeinschaft und Gesellschaft. Translated and Edited by Charles P. Loomis* TB/1116

SAMUEL E. WALLACE: Skid Row as a Way of Life TB/1367

W. LLOYD WARNER and Associates: Democracy in Jonesville: *A Study in Quality and Inequality* || TB/1129

W. LLOYD WARNER: Social Class in America: *The Evaluation of Status* TB/1013

FLORIAN ZNANIECKI: The Social Role of the Man of Knowledge. *Introduction by Lewis A. Coser* TB/1372

11